GoodFood
101 Picnics & packed lunches

Editor **Sharon Brown**

Contents

Introduction

There's nothing better on a sunny summer's day than packing up a picnic and taking off to the beach, park or riverside to enjoy eating in the great outdoors. Maybe it's a family get-together or a summer birthday, but whatever the event what you need is delicious, easily portable food.

It's also worth remembering that homemade packed lunches make perfect sense too, whether they are to take to school, college or work. It's much cheaper to make your own salads and snacks to pack up, and it's easier to make healthier choices when you're not relying on pricey, high-fat, shop-bought items that often don't even taste as good as your own culinary creations.

We've chosen a tempting range of pasties, tarts, hearty salads and easy-make sides so you can mix and match the picnic or lunch of your choice, plus we've included some sweet treats too. It's important to keep foods chilled, so a cool box or bag is your picnic's best friend, and they come in all shapes and sizes and even with wheels – so there's no reason not to take one! Remember to freeze some cool packs the night before to pop into your box. Also, if you're enjoying the recipes from this book outside in the fresh air, don't forget the picnic essentials: sharp knife, small chopping board, kitchen roll, a bag for rubbish and a bottle opener.

All the recipes here have been triple-tested by the *Good Food* team and are guaranteed to be easy to cook and delicious to eat. And, of course, like the best picnic food, all these dishes travel well, whether you're off to work or all set to enjoy a day out and about.

Sharon

Sharon Brown
Good Food magazine

Notes and conversion tables

NOTES ON THE RECIPES
- Eggs are large in the UK and Australia and extra large in America unless stated otherwise.
- Wash fresh produce before preparation.
- Recipes contain nutritional analyses for 'sugar', which means the total sugar content including all natural sugars in the ingredients, unless otherwise stated.

OVEN TEMPERATURES

Gas	°C	°C Fan	°F	Oven temp.
¼	110	90	225	Very cool
½	120	100	250	Very cool
1	140	120	275	Cool or slow
2	150	130	300	Cool or slow
3	160	140	325	Warm
4	180	160	350	Moderate
5	190	170	375	Moderately hot
6	200	180	400	Fairly hot
7	220	200	425	Hot
8	230	210	450	Very hot
9	240	220	475	Very hot

APPROXIMATE WEIGHT CONVERSIONS
- All the recipes in this book list both imperial and metric measurements. Conversions are approximate and have been rounded up or down. Follow one set of measurements only; do not mix the two.
- Cup measurements, which are used by cooks in Australia and America, have not been listed here as they vary from ingredient to ingredient. Kitchen scales should be used to measure dry/solid ingredients.

Good Food is concerned about sustainable sourcing and animal welfare. Where possible, humanely reared meats, sustainably caught fish (see fishonline.org for further information from the Marine Conservation Society) and free-range chickens and eggs are used when recipes are originally tested.

SPOON MEASURES

Spoon measurements are level unless otherwise specified.

- 1 teaspoon (tsp) = 5ml
- 1 tablespoon (tbsp) = 15ml
- 1 Australian tablespoon = 20ml (cooks in Australia should measure 3 teaspoons where 1 tablespoon is specified in a recipe)

APPROXIMATE LIQUID CONVERSIONS

metric	imperial	AUS	US
50ml	2fl oz	¼ cup	¼ cup
125ml	4fl oz	½ cup	½ cup
175ml	6fl oz	¾ cup	¾ cup
225ml	8fl oz	1 cup	1 cup
300ml	10fl oz/½ pint	½ pint	1¼ cups
450ml	16fl oz	2 cups	2 cups/1 pint
600ml	20fl oz/1 pint	1 pint	2½ cups
1 litre	35fl oz/1¾ pints	1¾ pints	1 quart

Tomato & pepper dip

This is a great choice for a first course because it's filling, but low in fat and calories. It has a bit of a kick to wake up the tastebuds, too!

TAKES 10 MINUTES • SERVES 12

375g jar Peppadew sweet piquant
   peppers, drained and rinsed
3 tomatoes, roughly chopped
1 tbsp sun-dried tomato paste
bunch chives, snipped

TO SERVE

selection of raw veg, such as cherry
   tomatoes, celery, spring onion,
   cucumber, peppers and carrots
soft flour tortillas

1 Tip the peppers, tomatoes, tomato paste and most of the chives into a food processor. Whizz together until blended, but still chunky.

2 Season with freshly ground black pepper and spoon into a serving dish. Sprinkle over the remaining chives and serve with lots of crisp, fresh raw veg sticks. Pop the soft flour tortillas under a hot grill for about a minute each, turning once until crisp, then snap them into pieces and serve with the dip.

PER SERVING 80 kcals, protein 1g, carbs 5g, fat 6g, sat fat 1g, fibre 2g, sugar none, salt 0.76g

Lemon & coriander houmous

This classic superhealthy dip is a popular favourite and counts as one of your 5-a-day.
Serve with fresh vegetable sticks, such as carrots, peppers and cucumber.

TAKES 5 MINUTES • SERVES 6

2 × 400g cans chickpeas in water,
    drained
2 fat garlic cloves, roughly chopped
3 tbsp Greek yogurt
3 tbsp tahini paste
3 tbsp extra virgin olive oil, plus extra
    to drizzle
zest and juice 2 lemons
20g pack coriander

1 Put everything but the coriander into a food processor, then whizz to a fairly smooth mix. Scrape down the sides of the processor, if you need to.

2 Season the houmous generously, then add the coriander and pulse until roughly chopped. Spoon into a serving bowl or pot with a lid, drizzle with oil, then serve or pack away and keep chilled for later.

PER SERVING 179 kcals, protein 7g, carbs 13g, fat 11g, sat fat 2g, fibre 6g, sugar 1g, salt 0.12g

Herby feta & lemon dip with crudités

Whipped feta takes on a creamy consistency in this delicious dip served with crunchy vegetables. Both the dip and vegetables can be prepared a day ahead.

TAKES 10–15 MINUTES ● **SERVES 6**

400g/14oz feta, drained and cut into chunks

juice 1 lemon

75ml/2½fl oz extra virgin olive oil

20g pack dill, roughly chopped

20g pack mint, finely chopped

FOR THE CRUDITÉS

selection of radishes, spring onions, cucumber batons and Cos lettuce leaves

1 Put the feta in a food processor or blender. Add the lemon juice and half the oil. Purée until smooth then add the remaining oil. Stir in the dill and mint.

2 Pour into a small container with a fitted lid and refrigerate until needed. Pack the veg in a shallow container and serve from the containers.

PER SERVING 282 kcals, protein 11g, carbs 3g, fat 25g, sat fat 10g, fibre 1g, sugar none, salt 2.45g

Best-ever chunky guacamole

The dip of all dips, this guacamole is the best ever because the ingredients have been kept to a minimum, so it is fresh tasting and vibrant.

TAKES 10 MINUTES • SERVES 8

1 large ripe tomato
3 avocados, very ripe but not bruised
juice 1 large lime
handful coriander, leaves and stalks
    chopped, plus a few leaves, roughly
    chopped, to garnish
1 small red onion, finely chopped
1 chilli, red or green, deseeded and
    finely chopped
tortilla chips or spicy potato wedges
    and soured cream, to serve

1 Use a large knife to pulverise the tomato to a pulp on a board, then tip into a bowl. Halve and stone the avocados (saving one stone) and use a spoon to scoop out the flesh into the bowl with the tomato.

2 Tip all the other ingredients into the bowl, then season with salt and freshly ground black pepper. Use a balloon whisk to roughly mash everything together as this keeps it lovely and chunky while still mashing it enough to make it into a dip. If not serving straight away, sit the stone in the guacamole (this helps to stop it going brown), cover with cling film and chill until needed. Scatter with the coriander, then serve with tortilla chips or spicy potato wedges and soured cream.

PER SERVING 103 kcals, protein 1g, carbs 2g, fat 10g, sat fat 1g, fibre 2g, sugar none, salt 0.01g

Spiced goat's cheese dip

This fresh tangy recipe is good for a picnic dip, or use it to spread on crackers or to stuff into pittas along with some salad.

TAKES 15 MINUTES • SERVES 4–6

1 tbsp sesame seeds
1 tsp cumin seeds
1 tsp coriander seeds
1 tbsp skinned hazelnuts
200g/7oz soft rindless goat's cheese
3–4 tbsp milk
few mint leaves, torn
radishes and bread, to serve

1 Put the seeds and nuts in a frying pan, then gently heat to toast them, removing them from the heat when the seeds start to pop and give off their aroma. Grind fairly coarsely using a pestle and mortar, then season with a little salt.

2 Beat the goat's cheese with the milk to soften it, then add a little seasoning, if needed. Tip half into a small bowl and scatter with half the ground seeds and a few torn mint leaves. Repeat the layers and serve the dip with a bowl of cold radishes and some bread.

PER SERVING (4) 145 kcals, protein 8g, carbs 2g, fat 12g, sat fat 5g, fibre none, sugar 1g, salt 0.62g

Smoky chipotle pepper salsa

This low-fat, spicy dip has a fabulous fresh flavour and makes a good summer snack or starter. Serve with crunchy tortilla chips.

TAKES ABOUT 20 MINUTES

● **SERVES 6**

2 red peppers, halved lengthways

6 ripe tomatoes, halved

1 garlic clove, crushed

juice 1 lime

1 tbsp extra virgin olive oil

2 tsp chipotle paste

1 red onion, finely chopped

20g pack coriander, roughly chopped

1 Heat grill to high. Put the peppers on to a baking sheet, skin-side up, and grill until the skins are black, then put into a bowl and cover. Leave until cool, then peel away and discard the skins.

2 Scoop out and discard the tomato seeds. Put the tomatoes into a food processor with the garlic, lime juice, oil and chipotle paste. Add the peppers, then pulse until chunky. Stir through the onion and coriander, then serve.

PER SERVING 55 kcals, protein 2g, carbs 8g, fat 2g, sat fat none, fibre 2g, sugar 7g, salt 0.06g

Smoked salmon & bean dip with crispy pittas

The pittas become crunchy in the oven, making them unbelievably moreish. Both the dip and pittas can be made the day before and packed separately to take to a picnic.

TAKES 30 MINUTES ● SERVES 8

FOR THE DIP

410g can cannellini beans, drained
   and rinsed
200g pot Greek yogurt
225g pack smoked salmon trimmings
1 tbsp chopped fresh dill
1 tbsp lemon juice

FOR THE PITTAS

6 pitta breads
2 tbsp olive oil
sea salt flakes
2 tbsp chopped fresh dill
2 bunches radishes, to serve

1 Tip the beans into a food processor with the yogurt and blend until smooth. Add the salmon and pulse, keeping the salmon quite chunky. Tip into a bowl and stir in the dill, lemon juice and a little seasoning.

2 To make the pittas, heat oven to 200C/180C fan/gas 6. Tear the pittas and spread out on two baking sheets. Drizzle with the oil and sprinkle with the sea salt and dill. Bake for 7 minutes until crisp, then leave to cool. Serve the dip with the crispy pittas and radishes.

PER SERVING 526 kcals, protein 7g, carbs 69g, fat 27g, sat fat 14g, fibre 2g, sugar 20g, salt 0.17g

Ham, tomato & watercress tart

The secret to this tempting tart is its cheesy, crisp polenta crust. You can make it up to 1 day ahead and keep it chilled.

TAKES 1 HOUR 10 MINUTES

● **SERVES 8**

FOR THE PASTRY

200g/7oz plain flour

50g/2oz fine polenta, plus extra for dusting

140g/5oz cold butter, cut into small pieces

50g/2oz Parmesan, finely grated

1 egg

FOR THE FILLING

4 eggs and 2 egg yolks

400ml/14fl oz double cream

150g pack smoked ham slices

100g/3½oz sun-dried tomatoes

handful watercress

1 Whizz the flour, polenta and butter in a food processor to fine breadcrumbs. Tip in the Parmesan and egg, then pulse through 2 tablespoons cold water until the mixture forms a ball. Wrap and chill for 30 minutes.

2 Dust a work surface with polenta. Roll out the pastry to fit a 28cm-round tart tin, with a little excess. Gently ease the pastry into the tin. Chill for 30 minutes.

3 Heat oven to 200C/180C fan/gas 6. Put some baking parchment on the pastry case and fill with baking beans. Bake for 15 minutes. Remove beans and parchment, then bake for 5 minutes. Trim away any overhanging pastry and put the pastry case on a baking sheet.

4 Reduce oven to 180C/160C fan/gas 4. Whisk together the eggs, yolks and cream. Arrange the ham, tomatoes and watercress in the case, then pour over the egg mixture. Cook for 30 minutes until the egg has set.

PER SERVING 631 kcals, protein 17g, carbs 31g, fat 50g, sat fat 27g, fibre 2g, sugar 3g, salt 2.61g

Smoked mackerel pâté with French bread & horseradish

This simple-to-make, no-cook pâté is always a popular treat. Any leftovers can be spread into sandwiches the next day, topped with cucumber.

TAKES 15 MINUTES ● SERVES 2

FOR THE PÂTÉ

25g/1oz unsalted butter, melted

zest ½ lemon

160g pack smoked mackerel (split fillets), skinned

1 spring onion, roughly chopped

FOR THE HORSERADISH BUTTER

15g/½oz unsalted butter, plus extra to serve

1 tsp hot horseradish sauce, plus extra to serve

1 tsp finely chopped flat-leaf parsley, plus a few extra leaves

French bread, to serve

1 Tip the melted butter, lemon zest, mackerel and spring onion into a food processor and blend until smooth. Spoon into small ramekins and smooth the top.

2 For the topping, melt the 15g butter with the horseradish, then stir in the parsley. Carefully spoon this mix over the pâté to cover it. Press some parsley leaves on top, grind over some black pepper and chill to set the butter. Serve the pâté with French bread, extra butter and horseradish sauce.

PER SERVING 440 kcals, protein 16g, carbs 1g, fat 41g, sat fat 17g, fibre 2g, sugar none, salt 2.26g

Country terrine with black pepper & thyme

Velvety chicken livers taste as though they should be expensive, yet are incredibly good value. This stunning terrine can be made and chilled up to 2 days ahead.

TAKES 1 HOUR 40 MINUTES, PLUS CHILLING • SERVES 8

butter, for greasing
750g/1lb 10oz streaky pork rashers
1 tbsp dried thyme
1 tsp black peppercorns
2 × 225g tubs frozen chicken livers, thawed
4 tbsp red or white wine
5 rashers smoked streaky bacon
cocktail gherkins or chutney and French bread, to serve

1 Heat oven to 180C/160C fan/gas 4 and butter a 1kg loaf tin. Roughly chop three of the pork rashers and mix with the thyme and peppercorns. Set aside. Put the remaining pork rashers into a food processor with two-thirds of the chicken livers, the wine and 1 teaspoon salt, then blend to a smooth pâté.

2 Spoon half the pâté into the tin, then top with the chopped pork mixture and remaining livers. Spoon the rest of the pâté mixture over the livers, then lay the bacon rashers over the top.

3 Cover the tin with foil and put in a roasting tin. Pour cold water into the roasting tin until it is half-filled, then bake for 1½ hours until the terrine is set. When cool, put another loaf tin on top and weigh it down to compress it. Leave overnight in the fridge. Slice the terrine and serve with gherkins or chutney and French bread.

PER SERVING 330 kcals, protein 30g, carbs none, fat 23g, sat fat 9g, fibre none, sugar none, salt 0.64g

Chicory with walnuts & Stilton

This combination of tempting flavours takes no time to prepare and can be made ahead. Just add the dressing before serving.

TAKES 20 MINUTES • SERVES 6

50g/2oz walnut pieces
3 large heads chicory
100g/3½oz Stilton

FOR THE DRESSING

1 tbsp walnut or hazelnut oil
3 tbsp sunflower oil
2 tbsp Dijon mustard
2 tbsp white wine vinegar
200ml/7fl oz single cream
crusty bread, to serve

1 To make the dressing, whisk the oils, mustard and vinegar together with a large pinch of salt and plenty of freshly ground black pepper. Pour in the cream in one go and stir with a spoon. Keep at room temperature until serving. (You can make the dressing up to 2 days ahead and chill in an airtight container.)

2 Heat a large pan over a high heat and throw in the walnuts. Toast for 10 minutes until they turn a deep golden colour, then tip out on to a plate and leave to cool. Cut the base off each chicory, then peel away the leaves. Wash, if necessary, and put on a large serving platter. Crumble over the cheese, pour over the dressing, then scatter with the toasted walnuts. Serve with a loaf of crusty bread.

PER SERVING 275 kcals, protein 7g, carbs 3g, fat 26g, sat fat 9g, fibre 1g, sugar 2g, salt 0.74g

Smoked salmon parcels with fennel & walnut salad

Salmon and walnuts make an unusual marriage, but the flavours and textures work really well together. These parcels would also make a great light lunch.

TAKES 20 MINUTES ● SERVES 4

350g/12oz smoked salmon
1 fennel bulb with fronds
2 rounded tbsp crème fraîche
3 tbsp lemon juice
5 tbsp walnut oil
few crisp lettuce leaves, such as
   Batavia or Little Gem
25g/1oz walnuts, roughly chopped

1 Select four slices of salmon and use to line four ramekins, allowing the slices to drape over the edges. Finely chop the remainder of the salmon and put in a bowl. Trim the fronds from the fennel and finely chop. Add the chopped fronds to the chopped salmon along with the crème fraîche, 1 tablespoon of the lemon juice and some seasoning. Mix well, then divide among the lined ramekins. Fold over any overhanging salmon and cover with cling film. Chill until ready to serve.

2 Halve, quarter and core the fennel bulb, then shred finely. Put in a bowl with the remaining lemon juice, 3 tablespoons of the walnut oil and some seasoning. Mix a few lettuce leaves on each plate and scatter over the dressed fennel. Invert the salmon parcels on to the plates, then scatter over the chopped walnuts. Drizzle with the remaining oil, season with black pepper and serve.

PER SERVING 329 kcals, protein 21g, carbs 2g, fat 27g, sat fat 6g, fibre 1g, sugar 2g, salt 3.6g

Pork & pistachio terrine

Terrines look impressive but are actually simple to put together. Wrap in foil and slice at the picnic for a stylish starter. Serve with red onion chutney and some cornichons.

TAKES 1 HOUR 35 MINUTES

● **SERVES 10**

12–18 rashers smoked streaky bacon

3 large garlic cloves, sliced

25g/1oz butter

800g/1lb 12oz minced pork

50g/2oz pistachio nuts

1 tsp salt

3 tbsp fresh thyme leaves

25g/1oz dried cranberries

3 tbsp brandy

1 egg, beaten

200g/7oz fresh chicken livers

1 Heat oven to 180C/160C fan/gas 4. Line a 900g loaf tin with 6–12 rashers of the bacon, slightly overlapping them and letting the excess hang over the top of the tin.

2 Fry the garlic in butter for just a minute, cool briefly, then mix with all the other ingredients except the livers. Season with plenty of black pepper.

3 Press half the mince mixture into the tin, then lay the livers on top. Cover with remaining mince mixture, then top with remaining rashers, cutting them in half for a neat fit. Fold over any bacon that is overhanging the tin.

4 Bake for 1¼ hours, then pour off most of the liquid, cover with foil and put a weight on top of the terrine as it cools to compact the texture (the easiest way is to use a couple of tins). As soon as it is cool enough, put it in the fridge.

PER SERVING 294 kcals, protein 25g, carbs 3g, fat 19g, sat fat 7g, fibre none, sugar 2g, salt 1.5g

Very easy pasta salad

This simple pasta dish can be quickly put together from storecupboard and freezer, and makes a great budget-friendly salad.

TAKES 12 MINUTES • SERVES 1

85g/3oz pasta shapes
3 tbsp frozen peas
3 tbsp frozen sweetcorn
1 tbsp natural yogurt
1 tbsp shop-bought balsamic dressing
1 tsp mayonnaise
1 tbsp chopped fresh basil
3 cherry tomatoes, halved

1 Cook the pasta shapes according to the pack instructions, adding the frozen peas and sweetcorn for the final minute. Drain and rinse in cold water.

2 Mix the yogurt and balsamic dressing with the mayonnaise. Pour on to the pasta, then stir through the chopped basil and cherry tomatoes, and toss together thoroughly.

PER SERVING 481 kcals, protein 14g, carbs 77g, fat 15g, sat fat 2g, fibre 5g, sugar 7g, salt 0.44g

Lemon potted crab

This delicious lemony pâté is good served with cheese straws or crunchy breadsticks, or partner it with chunks of wholemeal bread.

TAKES 15 MINUTES • SERVES 8
400g/14oz crab meat
large pinch cayenne pepper
zest and juice ½ lemon
300g/10oz butter
fresh parsley leaves, to garnish

1 Combine the crab, cayenne, lemon juice and zest, and season well. Pack into eight small ramekins or one large one, depending on what you have.
2 Melt the butter, then pour over the crab in the pot(s) until it is covered with a thin film. Top with a parsley leaf, then cool in the fridge. (This pâté will keep for up to 2 days in the fridge.) To prevent the butter melting, transport in a chiller bag.

PER SERVING 344 kcals, protein 10g, carbs none, fat 34g, sat fat 20g, fibre none, sugar none, salt 1.11g

Roasted chicken & new potato salad

Pack this superhealthy salad and dressing separately, and toss just before eating.
For a change, try using fresh chopped mint or coriander instead of the tarragon.

TAKES 25 MINUTES • SERVES 4

500g bag new potatoes, halved if large
1 ready-roasted chicken, about 900g
150g pot low-fat yogurt
1 tbsp clear honey
handful tarragon leaves, roughly
   chopped
225g bag salad leaves
4 roasted red peppers from a jar, sliced

1 Boil or steam the potatoes for 15–20 minutes until tender, then cool quickly in cold water (it's fine if they're still a bit warm) and drain. Meanwhile, pull the meat off the roast chicken and tear into bite-size pieces.

2 Mix the yogurt with the honey and tarragon, then season to taste. Toss the salad leaves, peppers, chicken and potatoes in a large bowl, drizzle the dressing over, then serve immediately.

PER SERVING 440 kcals, protein 37g, carbs 32g, fat 19g, sat fat 4g, fibre 3g, sugar 3g, salt 1.48g

Carrot & sesame burgers

These veggie burgers are much lighter than their meat-based cousins and are delicious cold. Pack the buns separately and assemble when you're ready to eat.

TAKES 50 MINUTES • MAKES 6

750g/1lb 10oz carrots, peeled and grated
410g can chickpeas, drained and rinsed
1 small onion, roughly chopped
2 tbsp tahini paste, plus 1 extra tsp
1 tsp ground cumin
1 egg
3 tbsp olive oil
100g/3½oz wholemeal breadcrumbs
zest 1 lemon, plus 1 tsp juice
3 tbsp sesame seeds
150g pot natural yogurt
6 bread buns, rocket leaves, sliced red onion, sliced avocado and chilli sauce, to serve

1 Put a third of the grated carrot in a food processor with the chickpeas, onion, tahini, cumin and egg. Whizz to a thick paste, then scrape into a bowl.

2 Heat 1 tablespoon of the oil in a pan, tip in the remaining carrot and cook for 8–10 minutes, until the carrot is soft. Add this to the whizzed paste along with the breadcrumbs, lemon zest and sesame seeds. Season, then mix with your hands.

3 Divide the mixture into six, then use wet hands to shape into burgers. Cover and chill until serving. Mix the yogurt with the extra tahini and the lemon juice, and chill.

4 Heat a non-stick frying pan and brush the burgers with the remaining oil. Cook for 5 minutes on each side, until golden and crisp. Meanwhile, toast the buns.

5 When you are ready to eat, spread each bun with some of the lemony sesame yogurt, add the burger, onion, avocado and chilli sauce, and serve.

PER BURGER 284 kcals, protein 10g, carbs 27g, fat 16g, sat fat 3g, fibre 7g, sugar 12g, salt 0.5g

Honey-mustard chicken pasta

There's a chance you'll already have most of the ingredients for this low-fat salad in your storecupboard and fridge. It's a good way to use up leftover roast chicken.

TAKES 20 MINUTES ● SERVES 4

300g/10oz farfalle or other pasta shape

3 tbsp reduced-fat mayonnaise (use
    full-fat, if you prefer)

1 heaped tsp wholegrain mustard

1 tsp clear honey

300g/10oz cooked chicken, torn into
    rough pieces

4 spring onions, thinly sliced (or
    ½ red onion, thinly sliced)

small bunch basil, leaves roughly torn

4 tomatoes, quartered, then each
    chunk halved

1 Cook the pasta according to the pack instructions, then cool under running water. Mix the mayonnaise, mustard and honey in a large bowl and loosen with a little water to make a dressing the consistency of double cream.

2 Add the pasta, chicken, onions, basil and tomatoes, season to taste, then gently mix together.

PER SERVING 450 kcals, protein 31g, carbs 62g, fat 11g, sat fat 3g, fibre 3g, sugar 6g, salt 0.55g

Greek salad wraps

All the flavours of Greece combine in these fresh-tasting snacks. Perfect for a picnic or lunch in the garden.

TAKES 10 MINUTES • SERVES 2

1 large vine-ripened tomato
50cm piece cucumber
6 pitted Kalamata olives (optional)
2 very large soft tortilla wraps
50g/2oz feta, cubed
2 heaped tbsp houmous

1 Roughly chop the tomato, cut the cucumber into sticks and split and stone the olives (if using).

2 Now heat the tortillas. If you have gas, put each one for 10 seconds on a lit gas ring (you have to be a little bit brave) then turn it over quickly, using tongs, and heat the other side for another 8 seconds. The tortillas will be slightly charred in places, which adds a fantastic flavour. Alternatively, warm a pan to a medium heat before quickly tossing in your tortillas one at a time.

3 Make a row of tomato, cucumber, feta and olives (if using) down the centre of each warm tortilla. Now spread the houmous around the top and sides of the tortilla. Fold in the sides to seal in the ingredients and roll up tightly to make a big cigar. Cut in half and eat with your fingers.

PER SERVING 297 kcals, protein 10g, carbs 25g, fat 18g, sat fat 5g, fibre 3g, sugar none, salt 2.08g

Prawn sweet-chilli noodle salad

Save money by making your own tasty take-to-work salad. This one has a spicy kick to it – just keep it cool until lunchtime.

TAKES 15 MINUTES ● SERVES 4–6

3 nests medium egg noodles
½ large cucumber
bunch spring onions, finely sliced
100g/3½oz cherry tomatoes, halved
1 green chilli, deseeded, finely chopped
200g/7oz bag cooked peeled king
    prawns, defrosted if frozen
zest and juice 2 limes
4 tbsp sweet chilli sauce
100g bag baby leaf spinach
25g/1oz roasted cashew nuts

1 Boil the noodles for 4 minutes, then drain. Cool under running water, then drain again. Put into a large bowl and then, using scissors, cut the noodles into shorter lengths.

2 Halve the cucumber lengthways, then scoop out the seeds. Slice into half-moons and add to the noodles with the onions, tomatoes, chilli and prawns.

3 Mix the lime zest, juice and chilli sauce to make a dressing and fold through the noodles. Add a handful of spinach to each plate and top with the noodles and cashews.

PER SERVING (4) 267 kcals, protein 20g, carbs 39g, fat 5g, sat fat 1g, fibre 5g, sugar 12g, salt 2.18g

Mini chicken pies

These lovely little pies are crisp outside and succulent inside and are ideal for a packed lunch or picnic. Children love them.

TAKES 40 MINUTES • MAKES 8

500g pack shortcrust pastry
2 cooked chicken breasts, shredded
85g/3oz peas, fresh or frozen
½ bunch asparagus, trimmed and cut
   into bite-size pieces
100ml/3½fl oz crème fraîche
1 egg, beaten

1 Roll out the pastry until a little thinner than a £1 coin. Cut out 8 × 9cm circles and use to line eight holes of a muffin tin. Divide the chicken, peas and asparagus among the pastry cases, season, then dollop 1 tablespoon of the crème fraîche over each.

2 Cut out 8 × 7cm circles to make tops for the pies. Lightly brush the edges of the pie bases with egg, put each top on to its pie and press down into the filling. Pinch together the sides to seal. Leave to rest in the fridge for 30 minutes, or up to 2 days, if preparing in advance.

3 Heat oven to 200C/180C fan/gas 6. Brush pie tops with more egg and bake for 30–35 minutes or until the pastry is crisp and golden. Can be served warm or leave until cold.

PER PIE 396 kcals, protein 15g, carbs 30g, fat 25g, sat fat 12g, fibre 2g, sugar 1g, salt 0.34g

Wild rice & feta salad

This fill-you-up recipe is great chilled for a lunchbox or served warm for a light supper. The fruitiness of the cranberries works well with the tangy cheese.

TAKES 30 MINUTES ● SERVES 4

250g/9oz mixed basmati and wild rice
400g can chickpeas, drained and rinsed
100g pack dried cranberries
1 red onion, sliced
1 garlic clove, crushed
3 tbsp olive oil
2 tbsp lemon juice
200g pack reduced-fat feta
handful flat-leaf parsley, roughly
    chopped, to garnish

1 Rinse the rice and cook according to the pack instructions, adding the chickpeas for the final 4 minutes. Drain and allow to cool a little, then mix through the cranberries and onion.
2 Whisk together the garlic, oil, lemon juice and seasoning to make a dressing. Toss with the rice mixture, then pile on to a large serving plate. Crumble over the feta, then scatter with parsley. Serve warm or cold.

PER SERVING 519 kcals, protein 20g, carbs 79g, fat 16g, sat fat 5g, fibre 4g, sugar 19g, salt 1.82g

Asparagus, sun-dried tomato & olive loaf

This savoury bake is brilliant served sliced and popped into a picnic hamper or lunchbox. Asparagus is a good source of folic acid and vitamin C.

TAKES 1 HOUR ● CUTS INTO 10 SLICES

100ml/3½fl oz olive oil, plus extra
    for greasing
250g/9oz asparagus spears, each
    cut into 3 pieces
200g/7oz self-raising flour
1 tbsp thyme leaves
3 eggs, lightly beaten
100ml/3½fl oz milk
handful pitted black olives
100g/3½oz sun-dried tomatoes,
    roughly chopped
100g/3½oz Gruyère or Beaufort, grated

1 Heat oven to 190C/170C fan/gas 5. Oil and line the base of a 900g loaf tin (approx 22 × 10 × 5cm) with baking parchment. Cook the asparagus in boiling, salted water for 2 minutes, drain, then cool quickly under cold running water. Pat dry.

2 Mix the flour and thyme with some seasoning in a large bowl. Make a well in the centre, then add the eggs, milk and oil, stirring all the time to draw the flour into the centre. Beat for 1 minute to make a smooth batter.

3 Reserve five asparagus tips and a few olives. Add the remaining asparagus and olives, the tomatoes and two-thirds of the cheese to the batter. Pour into the tin, then put the reserved asparagus and olives on top. Sprinkle with the remaining cheese. Bake for 35–40 minutes until the loaf feels firm and is golden and crusty on top. Cool in the tin for 5 minutes, then turn out and cool on a wire rack.

PER SLICE 317 kcals, protein 11g, carbs 22g, fat 21g, sat fat 5g, fibre 3g, sugar 3g, salt 1.04g

Chicken roll-ups

These wraps are so simple that children can make their own with no problems.
For a change, replace the chicken with ham or salami and add cucumber or lettuce.

TAKES 10 MINUTES ● MAKES 1

1–2 tbsp houmous
1 wrap or tortilla
3 fat slices cooked chicken breast
¼ avocado, sliced
3 cherry tomatoes, quartered
1 tbsp grated Cheddar

1 Spread the houmous over the middle of the wrap. Tear up the chicken and arrange down the centre of the wrap with the avocado slices.
2 Top with the tomatoes and sprinkle over the grated cheese. Roll up the wrap and press firmly. Cut in half to serve.

PER ROLL-UP 428 kcals, protein 28g, carbs 31g, fat 22g, sat fat 5g, fibre 4g, sugar 2g, salt 1.03g

Tortellini with pesto & broccoli

This tasty, satisfying meal can be made ahead in just 10 minutes – perfect to pop into a lunchbox for work, school or college.

TAKES 10 MINUTES ● SERVES 2

140g/5oz Tenderstem broccoli, cut into short lengths
250g pack fresh tortellini (ham and cheese works well)
3 tbsp pesto (fresh if you can get it)
2 tbsp toasted pine nuts
1 tbsp balsamic vinegar
8 cherry tomatoes, halved

1 Bring a large pan of water to the boil. Add the broccoli, cook for 2 minutes, then add the tortellini and cook for 2 minutes, or according to the pack instructions. Drain everything, gently rinse under cold water until cool, then tip into a bowl.

2 Add the pesto, pine nuts and balsamic vinegar to the bowl and toss together. Add the tomatoes, pack into containers and chill. Let the salad get to room temperature throughout the morning to get the most flavour from the tomatoes and pesto.

PER SERVING 573 kcals, protein 24g, carbs 64g, fat 26g, sat fat 9g, fibre 5g, sugar 8g, salt 1.58g

From-the-fridge omelette

You can use whatever veg you have to hand for this delicious omelette – aubergine, sweet potato, tomato and cooked potato are all good choices.

TAKES 15 MINUTES ● SERVES 4

1 tbsp olive oil

1 courgette, sliced

4 eggs

½ teacup (about 125g/4½oz) frozen peas (no need to defrost)

handful grated or sliced cheese (Cheddar, feta, ricotta or goat's cheese work well)

1 Heat the oil in your smallest non-stick frying pan (around 20cm). Tip in the courgette and cook for a couple of minutes, just until it starts to turn golden. Beat the eggs in a bowl with a little seasoning.

2 Add the peas to the pan, then pour in the eggs and sprinkle with the cheese. Turn the heat down really low and cook for about 10 minutes until the egg has almost set. In the meantime, heat the grill to high.

3 After 10 minutes on the hob, pop the pan under the hot grill for a minute or two until all the egg has set. Put a cutting board or plate over the pan and flip over. Cut the omelette into four wedges and serve warm, or leave to cool and serve with salad or coleslaw. (Can be kept in the fridge for up to 3 days.)

PER SERVING 175 kcals, protein 12g, carbs 2g, fat 13g, sat fat 5g, fibre 1g, sugar 1g, salt 0.40g

Turkey & bacon club

If you grill the bacon and butter the bread the night before, all you need to do the next day is assemble and eat.

TAKES 15 MINUTES • MAKES 1

2 streaky bacon rashers

butter, for spreading

3 slices bread (white or brown, or a mix)

1 thick slice cooked turkey

a little mayonnaise and mustard

few lettuce leaves, shredded

½ avocado, sliced

1 Grill the bacon until crisp, then drain on kitchen paper. Butter one slice of bread on one side, then cover with the turkey, a little mayonnaise and the shredded lettuce.

2 Butter both sides of the next slice of bread, then put on top of the turkey. Spread a little mustard over the bread, then arrange the bacon on top, with the sliced avocado. Butter the last slice of bread and put on top. Press the sandwich down lightly, then cut in half.

PER SANDWICH 745 kcals, protein 31g, carbs 54g, fat 46g, sat fat 19g, fibre 4g, sugar 4g, salt 3.44g

Big American salad

You can use any dressing you've got for this salad. Packed with goodness, it's low in fat and easy enough for the kids to help put together.

TAKES 30 MINUTES • SERVES 4

250g pack smoked streaky bacon rashers

250g pack prepared French beans

1 large Cos lettuce, shredded and washed

1 small red onion, halved and finely sliced

2 × 250g packs cherry tomatoes, finely sliced

1 fennel bulb, finely sliced

½ cucumber, finely sliced

125g pack baby button mushrooms

100g/3½oz black olives, stoned

100g/3½oz frozen peas, rinsed in warm water

2 large cooked chicken breasts, skinned and shredded

2 × 60g packs toasted croûtons

1 Heat the grill. Bring a pan of water to the boil. Grill the bacon until crisp. Cook the beans for 3 minutes or until tender, cool under a cold tap, then cut in half.

2 Take a big, wide container and spread the lettuce in the bottom. Scatter over the onion, tomatoes, fennel, cucumber and mushrooms, then jumble them together. Break the bacon into big pieces, mix with the olives, peas, chicken, croûtons and beans, then scatter over. Cover and store in the fridge (keeps for a day) ready for a picnic or lunchboxes.

PER SERVING 233 kcals, protein 22g, carbs 18g, fat 9g, sat fat 3g, fibre 5g, sugar none, salt 2.29g

Ham, pea & mint pasties

Pasties have been given an update with this recipe – a really fresh taste of summer with a light ricotta, ham and minty-pea filling.

TAKES 1 HOUR 40 MINUTES
● **MAKES 4**
FOR THE PASTRY
175g/6oz cold butter, chopped into chunks
350g/12oz plain flour, plus extra for dusting
½ tsp English mustard powder
1 beaten egg, to glaze
FOR THE FILLING
50g/2oz butter
1 onion, finely chopped
200g/7oz peas, frozen or cooked fresh
100g/3½oz thickly sliced ham, chopped into small chunks
small bunch mint, leaves picked and finely chopped
250g pack ricotta

1 Whizz the butter, flour and mustard for the pastry in a food processor with ½ teaspoon salt. Add 4–5 tablespoons cold water, a spoonful at a time, while pulsing until the pastry comes together. Bring together into a ball and chill.
2 Melt the butter in a pan. Gently sweat the onion for 10–15 minutes until really soft. Stir in the peas for 1 minute, then turn off the heat and stir in the ham chunks, chopped mint and ricotta with plenty of seasoning.
3 Heat oven to 180C/160C fan/gas 4. Divide the pastry into four pieces. Roll each piece to a neat 16–17cm circle (cut round a saucer). Brush the edges with some of the beaten egg, spoon a quarter of the filling into the middle, then bring up opposite sides of pastry together and seal. Crimp to make a pasty shape. Lift on to a baking sheet. Repeat the process for the remaining pasties. Bake for 35–40 minutes until golden, then serve.

PER PASTY 919 kcals, protein 25g, carbs 79g, fat 58g, sat fat 35g, fibre 6g, sugar 6g, salt 1.76g

Salmon & egg wraps with mustard mayo

A great idea when entertaining a crowd. For veggies, you can swap the salmon for strips of roasted red peppers from a jar.

TAKES 20 MINUTES ● MAKES 12

24 slices smoked salmon
6 hard-boiled eggs, cooled, shelled and
  sliced
2 × 100g bags baby leaf spinach
12 large wraps (we used multigrain)

FOR THE MUSTARD MAYO

200g/7oz light mayonnaise
6 tbsp Dijon mustard
1 small red onion, very finely sliced

1 Mix the mayonnaise and mustard, divide into two small bowls, then stir the onion into one bowl.
2 Spread a layer of the onion mayonnaise over each wrap and add two slices of the smoked salmon, some sliced hard-boiled egg and a generous helping of spinach to each. Roll up tightly. The wraps can be made several hours ahead and kept covered in the fridge. To serve, cut each wrap on the diagonal into two pieces. Serve with the extra mustard mayo for drizzling.

PER WRAP 356 kcals, protein 23g, carbs 35g, fat 15g, sat fat 3g, fibre 3g, sugar 3g, salt 4.31g

Asian chicken salad

Great for a lunchbox, or double up this recipe and serve it for a summer family lunch; the zingy flavours will wake up the tastebuds.

TAKES 20 MINUTES • SERVES 2

1 boneless, skinless chicken breast
1 tbsp fish sauce
zest and juice ½ lime (about 1 tbsp)
1 tsp caster sugar
100g bag mixed leaves
large handful fresh coriander,
   roughly chopped
¼ red onion, thinly sliced
½ chilli, deseeded and thinly sliced
¼ cucumber, halved lengthways, sliced

1 Cover the chicken with cold water, bring to the boil, then cook for 10 minutes. Remove from the pan and tear into shreds. Stir together the fish sauce, lime zest, juice and sugar until the sugar dissolves.

2 Put the leaves and coriander in a container, then top with the chicken, onion, chilli and cucumber. Put the dressing in a separate container and toss through the salad when ready to eat.

PER SERVING 109 kcals, protein 19g, carbs 6g, fat 1g, sat fat none, fibre 1g, sugar 5g, salt 1.6g

Creamy salmon & sugar snap pasta

A good source of omega-3 and vitamin C, you'll love this classic combination. You could use flakes of hot-smoked salmon or trout instead.

TAKES 15 MINUTES ● SERVES 4

400g/14oz fusilli pasta or other pasta shape

150g pack sugar snap peas, halved lengthways

2 salmon steaks (300g/10oz total)

zest and juice ½ lemon

4 tbsp reduced-fat crème fraîche

100g bag rocket leaves

1 Cook the pasta according to the pack instructions, adding the sugar snaps to the water 2 minutes before the cooking time is up. Cool under cold running water, then drain. You can steam the salmon over the pasta pan for about 7 minutes if you have a steamer basket, or put it on to a heatproof plate and microwave on High for 2–3 minutes until the flesh flakes easily. Peel away any skin, break into large flakes, then allow to cool.

2 Mix the lemon zest, juice and crème fraîche together, then season to taste. If you need to, loosen with a few tablespoons of water to make it the consistency of double cream. Toss the pasta, peas and rocket into the dressing, flake in the salmon, then gently turn in the bowl a few times.

PER SERVING 527 kcals, protein 30g, carbs 79g, fat 13g, sat fat 3g, fibre 4g, sugar 4g, salt 0.14g

Orzo & mozzarella salad

Orzo is a very small pasta shape available in large supermarkets. If you can't find it, use any other tiny pasta, like stelline (small stars) or rice-shaped risoni.

TAKES 18 MINUTES • SERVES 4

350g/12oz orzo

20g pack basil

4 tbsp extra virgin olive oil

25g/1oz Parmesan, finely grated, plus more to garnish (optional)

1 garlic clove, very roughly chopped

50g/2oz toasted pine nuts

290g pack bocconcini (baby mozzarella balls)

100g/3½oz semi-dried tomatoes, roughly chopped

50g bag rocket leaves

1 Boil the orzo for 8 minutes until tender, then drain and cool under cold water. Drain again, then tip into a large bowl. Meanwhile, tear the basil, stalks and all, into a food processor. Add the oil, Parmesan, garlic and half the pine nuts, then whizz to a thick pesto-like consistency for the dressing.

2 Stir the dressing through the orzo, then season. The dressing will seem quite thick, but keep stirring and it will eventually coat all the grains. Add the bocconcini, tomatoes and a handful of rocket. Scatter with the remaining pine nuts and a little more Parmesan, if you like. Top with more rocket, then serve.

PER SERVING 742 kcals, protein 29g, carbs 71g, fat 40g, sat fat 13g, fibre 4g, sugar 5g, salt 1.25g

Quiche Lorraine frittata

You should have almost all these ingredients, or similar, to hand, so there's no shopping required. Simply serve with salad or stuff into bread and you're ready to go.

TAKES 40 MINUTES ● SERVES 6

8 rashers smoked streaky bacon or
    about 175g/6oz cooked ham,
    chopped into pieces
8 eggs
200ml/7fl oz milk
50g/2oz strong Cheddar, grated, plus
    extra for sprinkling (optional)
cherry tomatoes and mixed leaves,
    to serve

1 Heat oven to 180C/160C fan/gas 4. If you're using bacon, put it into a large frying pan and cook over a gentle-medium heat. Stir occasionally until golden and beginning to crisp up.

2 Line a roasting tin, about 20 × 28cm, with baking parchment – just scrunch it roughly at the corners. Whisk together the eggs and milk in a large jug or bowl, then stir in the bacon or ham, plus any fat from the pan, the Cheddar and some seasoning. Pour into the tin, scatter with a bit of extra grated cheese, if you like, and bake for 30–35 minutes until golden and set. Carry to your picnic in its tin and eat hot, warm or cold, with bread, cherry tomatoes and a few salad leaves.

PER SERVING 229 kcals, protein 17g, carbs 2g, fat 17g, sat fat 6g, fibre none, sugar 2g, salt 1.3g

Satay chicken pieces

These aromatic Thai-flavoured drumsticks and thighs are perfect with sweet chilli sauce or mango chutney – finger-lickin' treats for a feast in the great outdoors.

TAKES 1 HOUR 10 MINUTES, PLUS MARINATING • SERVES 6

6 skinless chicken drumsticks and 6 skinless chicken thighs
zest and juice 1 lime
2 lemongrass stalks, very roughly chopped
2 thumb-size chunks fresh root ginger, very roughly chopped
3 garlic cloves
2 tbsp peanut butter, crunchy or smooth
½ tsp each ground turmeric and ground cumin
160ml can coconut cream
20g pack coriander, plus extra leaves to garnish
a little oil, for greasing
sweet chilli sauce or mango chutney, to serve

1 Slash several deep cuts into each drumstick and thigh, then put into a large, non-metallic container. Put the lime zest and juice, lemongrass, ginger, garlic, peanut butter, spices, coconut cream and 1 teaspoon salt into a food processor, then whizz until it's smooth. Roughly chop the coriander leaves and finely chop the stalks, then add to the mix. Pour the marinade over the chicken, rub it in with your hands, then leave to chill for at least 2 hours, or up to 24 hours, if you have time.

2 Heat oven to 190C/170C fan/gas 5. Line one or two large baking sheets with foil and grease with a little oil. Spread the chicken over the sheets, skin-side up, and roast for 1 hour, until the chicken is cooked through, golden, and slightly charred in places. Cool, then chill and pack in a container, ready to transport. Scatter with a few more coriander leaves and serve with the sauce or chutney.

PER SERVING 302 kcals, protein 34g, carbs 3g, fat 17g, sat fat 10g, fibre none, sugar 2g, salt 0.4g

Wholemeal spinach & potato pies

The creamy potato, cheese and spinach filling makes these a really moreish treat for vegetarians. They're great served warm or cold.

TAKES 1 HOUR 20 MINUTES
- **MAKES 8**

140g/5oz plain wholemeal flour
140g/5oz plain white flour, plus extra
    for dusting
85g/3oz cold butter, diced
85g/3oz shredded vegetable suet
up to 100ml/3½fl oz milk
1 egg, beaten, to glaze

FOR THE FILLING

1 small baking potato, peeled and cut
    into small chunks
200g/7oz spinach leaves
150ml pot single cream
1 egg, beaten
100g/3½oz Cheddar, grated
grated fresh nutmeg

1 Rub the flours together with the butter and suet to make breadcrumbs, then work in the milk until the pastry comes together. Knead until soft, then wrap and chill for 1 hour.

2 Boil the potato for 10 minutes until cooked, then drain well. Tip the spinach into a colander, pour over boiling water, then squeeze out all the liquid. In a bowl, mix the spinach with the potato, cream, egg and two-thirds of the cheese. Season with salt, pepper and nutmeg. Heat oven to 200C/180C fan/gas 6.

3 Roll out the pastry on a floured surface to thickness of a £1 coin. Cut out eight squares approximately 13 × 13cm. Spoon the filling mix into the centre of each square, then brush the edges with egg. Bring all four corners together over the filling, pinching the edges together.

4 Transfer to a baking sheet. Brush each pie with egg, then top with remaining cheese. Bake for 30 minutes until golden, then leave to cool slightly.

PER PIE 421 kcals, protein 11g, carbs 31g, fat 31g, sat fat 11g, fibre 3g, sugar 2g, salt 0.57g

Scotch eggs

A classic and a favourite with all the family. Homemade Scotch eggs are so much tastier than shop-bought ones. These can be cooked the day before and chilled.

TAKES 40 MINUTES ● MAKES 8

400g/14oz pork sausagemeat or
   8 good-quality sausages, split from
   their skins
large handful parsley, chopped
large handful coriander, chopped
1 tsp English mustard powder
8 hard-boiled eggs
250g/9oz breadcrumbs
sunflower oil, for frying

1 Put the sausagemeat in a bowl with the herbs, mustard, some seasoning and 4 tablespoons water, and mix really well. Using your hands, coat each egg with a layer, roughly 5cm thick, of the sausage mixture. Now roll the eggs in the breadcrumbs until completely coated.

2 Heat a 5cm depth of oil in a small saucepan and, once it is shimmering on the surface, fry the eggs two at a time for 6 minutes, turning as they brown. Remove with a slotted spoon and drain on kitchen paper.

PER SCOTCH EGG 414 kcals, protein 17g, carbs 29g, fat 26g, sat fat 7g, fibre 1g, sugar 2g, salt 1.73g

Herb-rolled pork loin with crackling

This is based on an Italian classic for suckling pig. It can be roasted up to 2 days ahead and kept in the fridge, tightly wrapped in foil.

TAKES 2½ HOURS ● SERVES 10

2 tbsp finely chopped rosemary
4 garlic cloves, finely chopped
2 tbsp fennel seeds
3 tbsp olive oil, plus extra for greasing
2.5kg/5lb 8oz boneless pork loin, butterflied (ask the butcher to do this for you)

1 Tip the rosemary, garlic, fennel, oil and a pinch of salt into a mortar and pound to a rough paste. Unfold the pork loin, spread the herb mixture all over the cut side, then fold the loin back over. Tie pieces of string around the loin at 2cm intervals and tuck any leftover rosemary sprigs under the string.

2 Heat oven to 220C/200C fan/gas 7. Put the pork on a lightly oiled baking sheet and sprinkle a little salt over the skin. Cook for 20 minutes until crisp and browned. Reduce oven to 190C/170C fan/gas 5 and cook for 45 minutes per kg more (which will be just under 2 hours for this amount of meat). When it's ready, remove the pork and cover tightly with foil. Leave to cool and keep in the fridge for up to 2 days. To serve, loosen the crackling then carve it into thick slices, handing out pieces of crackling.

PER SERVING 587 kcals, protein 54g, carbs 1g, fat 41g, sat fat 15g, fibre none, sugar none, salt 0.59g

Grilled vegetable bloomer

A perfect portable choice for lunch. If time is short you could use grilled and marinated veg from the deli counter instead of grilling your own.

TAKES 1 HOUR 10 MINUTES

● **CUTS INTO 12 WEDGES**

3 red peppers, halved and deseeded
2 yellow peppers, halved and deseeded
6 tbsp olive oil
1 aubergine, sliced into long strips
2 courgettes, sliced into long strips
800g/1¾lb bloomer loaf
1 red onion, sliced
2 tbsp good-quality fresh pesto
handful basil leaves

1 Heat oven to 220C/200C fan/gas 7. Put the peppers, cut-side down, on a baking sheet, drizzle with 2 tablespoons of the oil, then roast for 20 minutes to colour the skins. Remove from the oven, put in a bowl, cover with cling film and leave to cool. Once cold, remove the skins and leave to one side. Drizzle the aubergine and courgettes with the rest of the oil, then cook in batches on a griddle pan until marked on both sides. Set aside.

2 Slice the loaf in half horizontally and carefully hollow out the middle, leaving two empty shells. Build up the loaf by putting the vegetables in layers and scattering each layer with onion, pesto and basil leaves. Try to keep all the colours separate to create different-coloured layers. Replace the lid, wrap tightly in cling film, then put in the fridge. Cut into 12 neat wedges to serve.

PER WEDGE 168 kcals, protein 5g, carbs 22g, fat 7g, sat fat 1g, fibre 2g, sugar 6g, salt 0.49g

Cornish pasties

Just right for a picnic or lunchbox, served with pickle and tomatoes. The black pepper is essential in this recipe, giving the pasties their spicy kick.

TAKES 1 HOUR 20 MINUTES
- **MAKES 4**

FOR THE PASTRY

125g/4½oz butter, chilled and diced

125g/4½oz lard, diced

500g/1lb 2oz plain flour, plus extra for
    dusting

1 egg, beaten, to seal and glaze

FOR THE FILLING

350g/12oz beef skirt or chuck steak,
    finely chopped

1 large onion, finely chopped

2 medium potatoes, peeled and thinly
    sliced

175g/6oz swede, peeled and finely
    diced

1 tbsp freshly ground black pepper

1 Rub the butter and lard into the flour with a pinch of salt using your fingertips or a food processor, then blend in around 6 tablespoons cold water to make a firm dough. Cut into four, then chill for about 20 minutes.

2 Heat oven to 220C/200C fan/gas 7. Mix together the filling ingredients with 1 teaspoon salt. Roll out each piece of dough on a lightly floured surface to a round about 23cm wide – use a plate to trim it to shape. Firmly pack a quarter of the filling along the centre of each round, leaving a margin at each end. Brush the pastry edge with some of the egg, carefully draw up both sides so that they meet at the top, then pinch together to seal. Lift on to a non-stick baking sheet and brush with a little egg.

3 Bake for 10 minutes, then lower oven to 180C/160C fan/gas 4 and cook for 45 minutes more until golden. Great served warm or cold.

PER PASTY 1,174 kcals, protein 34g, carbs 114g, fat 68g, sat fat 35g, fibre 6g, sugar 7g, salt 1.96g

Spicy tiffin eggs

Vegetarians don't have to miss out on one of the summer picnic favourites – these eggs have a spicy carrot, crumb and cashew nut coating.

TAKES 40 MINUTES • MAKES 6

7 eggs
2 tbsp olive oil
1 onion, chopped
250g/9oz grated carrot
2 heaped tbsp korma curry paste
200g/7oz granary breadcrumbs
85g/3oz roasted cashews, finely
   chopped

1 Put six of the eggs in a pan of water and bring to the boil. Boil for 5 minutes, then cool in cold water. Carefully shell.
2 Heat the oil, fry the onion for 5 minutes, then add carrot and cook for 10 minutes until soft. Stir in the curry paste and fry for a few minutes more. Stir in the breadcrumbs, then, when the mixture is cool, beat the remaining egg and stir in to make a paste.
3 Divide the mixture into six and flatten with your hands (wetting them makes this easier), then use to wrap round each egg – the mixture will seal well as you press it together. Roll in the cashews and chill until ready to cook – the eggs can be kept in the fridge overnight.
4 Heat oven to 190C/170C fan/gas 5, then bake the eggs for 15–20 minutes. Leave to cool. Serve with mango chutney and salad.

PER TIFFIN EGG 340 kcals, protein 15g, carbs 24g, fat 21g, sat fat 4g, fibre 3g, sugar 6g, salt 0.77g

Big chicken & croûton salad

A shop-bought, ready-roasted chicken is a great summer cheat and means you can put this tempting main meal salad together in just 20 minutes.

TAKES 20 MINUTES • SERVES 4

1 ready-roasted chicken
2 thick slices ciabatta, sourdough or
    crusty white bread
1 tbsp olive oil
1 large Cos lettuce, shredded
1 celery stick, finely sliced
4 spring onions, finely chopped
½ cucumber, diced
90ml/3fl oz mayonnaise
1½ tbsp white wine or tarragon vinegar
small bunch tarragon, chopped

1 Remove the skin from the chicken and pull the meat off the bones in chunks. Tear the meat into smaller pieces. Toast the bread, brush with oil and roughly chop into chunky croûtons.

2 Put the lettuce into a large bowl and scatter over the chicken, celery, onions and cucumber in layers. (You can prepare until this stage up to 2 hours in advance, if you keep the salad in the fridge.)

3 Mix the mayonnaise with the vinegar and season well. Stir in the chopped tarragon, then spoon over the salad. Toss well, scatter with the croûtons and serve.

PER SERVING 726 kcals, protein 61g, carbs 18g, fat 46g, sat fat 12g, fibre 3g, sugar 5g, salt 4.1g

Pork & herb meatloaf

A tasty main course for a family picnic – serve simply with a crisp green salad and crusty bread. Any leftovers can be popped into lunchboxes.

TAKES 1 HOUR 20 MINUTES

● **CUTS INTO 8–10 SLICES**

2 slices fresh white bread, crusts removed

500g pack minced pork

1 onion, roughly chopped

1 garlic clove, roughly chopped

big handful parsley

1 tbsp fresh chopped oregano or 1 tsp dried

4 tbsp freshly grated Parmesan

1 egg, beaten

8 slices prosciutto

1 Heat oven to 190C/170C fan/gas 5. Put the bread in a food processor and blitz to make crumbs, then tip into a bowl with the pork. Tip the onion, garlic and herbs into the food processor and process until finely chopped. Add to the pork with the Parmesan and egg. Finely chop two slices of the prosciutto and add to the mix with some salt and pepper. Mix well.

2 Use the remaining prosciutto to line a 1.5-litre loaf tin. Spoon in the meatloaf mix and press down well. Flip the overhanging prosciutto over the top, then put the loaf tin into a roasting tin. Pour hot water into the roasting tin to come halfway up the sides of the loaf tin and bake for 1 hour until the loaf shrinks from the sides of the tin.

3 Cool in the tin for 10 minutes, then drain off any excess liquid and turn out on to a board. Cut into slices to serve.

PER SLICE (for 8) 180 kcals, protein 18g, carbs 5g, fat 10g, sat fat 4g, fibre 1g, sugar 1g, salt 0.63g

Mustard-crusted fillet of beef with deli salad

Impress friends and family with this luxurious beef fillet all-in-one dish – a stylish enough centrepiece for the smartest picnic.

TAKES 40–50 MINUTES ● SERVES 6

3 tbsp black peppercorns
2 tbsp sea salt
2 tbsp English mustard powder
1.25–1.5kg/2lb 12oz–3lb 5oz middle
    fillet of beef
3 tbsp olive oil
1kg/2lb 4oz baby new potatoes
50g/2oz butter
2 × 85g bags watercress
290g jar grilled artichoke hearts
200g tub marinated grilled red and
    yellow peppers
small handful mint leaves

1 Crush the peppercorns with a pestle and mortar then mix in the salt and mustard. Sprinkle on to a large plate. Brush the beef with some of the oil and roll in the seasoning.

2 Heat the remaining oil until very hot in a large heavy-based pan. Put the beef in the pan and turn the heat to medium. Sear for 30 minutes, turning every 6–7 minutes until the seasonings form a deep brown crust. This will be rare; for well cooked, add 10 minutes. Leave to cool. Boil the potatoes for 10–15 minutes until tender. Drain, toss in the butter.

3 To take to the picnic, put the potatoes in a foil parcel. Slice the beef thinly, transfer to a square of foil, pour over the juices and wrap. At the picnic, scatter watercress over a platter. Lay the beef over and scatter artichokes and peppers around. Drizzle over the oil from the artichoke jar and pour over the meat juices. Tear the mint over the warm potatoes and serve.

PER SERVING 571 kcals, protein 51g, carbs 34g, fat 26g, sat fat 7g, fibre 3g, sugar none, salt 3.34g

Roasted tomato & aubergine tart

Roasted cherry tomatoes top a basil-flavoured aubergine purée in this terrific cheesy tart – a great picnic main course for vegetarians. Serve with a crunchy salad.

TAKES 1½ HOURS • SERVES 6

FOR THE PASTRY

85g/3oz butter
175g/6oz plain flour
½ tsp paprika
½ tsp mustard powder
50g/2oz Gruyère cheese, grated
1 egg yolk

FOR THE FILLING

2 medium aubergines
450g/1lb cherry tomatoes
1 tbsp olive oil
2 garlic cloves, crushed
4 tbsp chopped fresh basil
crunchy salad leaves, to serve

1 Heat oven to 200C/180C fan/gas 6. Prick the aubergines all over, then bake for 45 minutes until soft.

2 Rub the butter into the flour in a bowl to fine breadcrumbs. Stir in the paprika, mustard, Gruyère and seasoning. Mix the egg yolk with 2 tablespoons cold water and mix into the flour to form a dough. Knead until smooth; wrap and chill.

3 Remove the aubergines from the oven and cool. Put the tomatoes in a roasting tin and pour over the oil. Roast for 10–15 minutes until just soft. Leave to cool. Halve the aubergines and scoop the flesh into a food processor. Add the garlic, basil and seasoning, then blend.

4 Roll out the pastry and use to line a 35 × 11cm tart tin. Prick the base, line with baking parchment and baking beans then bake blind for 10 minutes. Remove the parchment and beans. Spread the aubergine purée into the pastry case, then arrange the tomatoes on top.

PER SERVING 289 kcals, protein 7g, carbs 27g, fat 18g, sat fat 9g, fibre 3g, sugar none, salt 0.43g

Minted falafel with teriyaki dressing

Grill the pitta breads before you leave home and pack them separately to the falafel and dressing, then put them together when you are ready to eat.

TAKES 35 MINUTES • SERVES 6

2 × 400g cans chickpeas
3 tbsp olive oil
1 medium egg, beaten
2 garlic cloves, crushed
pinch chilli powder
½ tsp ground cumin
½ tsp ground coriander
4 tbsp chopped fresh mint
8 water biscuits, crushed

FOR THE DRESSING

4 tbsp tahini paste
4 tbsp olive oil
2 tbsp teriyaki marinade
2 tbsp lemon juice

TO SERVE

6 pitta breads
175g/6oz radicchio or other salad
    leaves, shredded

1 Drain and rinse the chickpeas and put in a food processor and process until finely ground. Add 1 tablespoon of the oil, the egg, garlic, spices, mint and seasoning to taste. Blend until smooth.

2 Add half the biscuits and blend again. If the paste looks as though it won't roll into balls at this stage, add more biscuits until the mix feels firm enough to handle. Divide the paste into about 20 pieces, roll into balls, then flatten each slightly. Heat the remaining oil in a frying pan and cook the falafel in batches for 3–4 minutes each side or until they are golden brown. Drain on kitchen paper.

3 Whisk all the dressing ingredients then add enough water to make a pouring consistency. Lightly grill the pitta breads and split to form pockets. Fill each pocket with radicchio or salad leaves and three or four falafel. Serve warm or cold, drizzled with the dressing.

PER SERVING 619 kcals, protein 21g, carbs 70g, fat 31g, sat fat 4g, fibre 8g, sugar none, salt 2.54g

Spiced pork & potato pie

This moneywise, satisfying pie can be eaten warm or is good cold for a picnic or sliced for a lunchbox, served with a selection of pickles.

TAKES 55 MINUTES • SERVES 6

1 medium potato, cut into chunks
1 tsp sunflower oil
500g pack lean minced pork
1 onion, finely chopped
1 garlic clove, chopped
¼ tsp each ground cinnamon, allspice
    and nutmeg
100ml/3½fl oz stock
400g/14oz ready-made shortcrust
    pastry
1 egg, beaten, to glaze

1 Heat oven to 200C/180C fan/gas 6. Boil the potato until tender, drain and mash, then leave to cool. Heat the oil in a non-stick pan, add the mince and onion, and quickly fry until browned. Add the garlic, spices, stock, plenty of freshly ground black pepper and a little salt and mix well. Remove from the heat, stir into the potato and leave to cool.

2 Roll out half the pastry and line the base of a 20–23cm pie plate or flan tin. Fill with the pork mixture and brush the edges of the pastry with water. Roll out the remaining dough and cover the pie. Press the edges of the pastry to seal, trimming off the excess. Prick the top of the pie to allow steam to escape and glaze the top with the beaten egg.

3 Bake for 30 minutes until the pastry is crisp and golden. Serve cut into wedges with a crisp green salad, or cold with a few pickles on the side.

PER SERVING 466 kcals, protein 26g, carbs 37g, fat 25g, sat fat 9g, fibre 2g, sugar 2g, salt 0.9g

Three-cheese bake

Never tried a savoury cheesecake before? Then go for it! It's perfect for a special summer picnic party and can be made ahead and frozen for up to 2 months.

TAKES 1¼ HOURS • SERVES 6

50g/2oz butter, melted, plus extra for greasing
150g/5½oz oatmeal biscuits
25g/1oz Parmesan, grated
2 × 250g tubs mascarpone cheese
2 medium eggs, beaten
150g/5½oz Stilton, cut into cubes

FOR THE SALAD

1 small head radicchio, torn
1 ripe pear, cored and thinly sliced
1 tbsp walnut oil
1 tsp white wine vinegar
50g/2oz toasted walnuts, roughly chopped

1 Heat oven to 190C/170C fan/gas 5. Lightly grease and base-line a 20cm springform tin. Crush the biscuits in a bag with a rolling pin until they resemble breadcrumbs. Pour the crumbs into a bowl and mix with the melted butter and Parmesan. Spoon into the prepared tin and press the mixture firmly into the base with the back of a spoon. Chill in the fridge for 15 minutes.

2 Meanwhile, beat together the mascarpone and eggs, and season well with black pepper. Fold in the Stilton and pour over the biscuit base. Smooth the surface and bake for 1 hour, covering the top with foil halfway through cooking, until lightly set and golden on top. Put on a wire rack to cool for 1 hour in the tin.

3 Toss all the salad ingredients together in a bowl and season to taste. Slice the cooled cheesecake into wedges and serve topped with the salad.

PER SERVING 781 kcals, protein 15g, carbs 14g, fat 75g, sat fat 39g, fibre 1g, sugar 4g, salt 1.65g

Chicken with goat's cheese & tarragon

This tastes rather special for something that's so simple to make. As an alternative to goat's cheese you can use Boursin.

TAKES 50 MINUTES • SERVES 8

8 skinless chicken breast fillets
20g pack tarragon
2 × 150g tubs soft goat's cheese
5 vine-ripened tomatoes
3 tbsp olive oil

1 Heat oven to 200C/180C fan/gas 6. Make a slit down the centre of each chicken breast with a sharp knife (taking care not to cut right through) then open up the slit to make a pocket. Arrange the chicken in a single layer in a large, lightly oiled ovenproof dish.

2 Reserve eight sprigs of tarragon, chop the rest of the leaves and beat into the cheese with plenty of ground black pepper. Spoon into the pockets in the chicken. Slice the tomatoes and put two slices over each cheese-filled pocket. Put a sprig of tarragon on top and drizzle with oil.

3 Season and bake for 25–30 minutes until the chicken is cooked, but still moist. To serve cold, pour off the juices otherwise they will set to a jelly once cold. Transport in the dish, covered with cling film.

PER SERVING 248 kcals, protein 34g, carbs 2g, fat 12g, sat fat 4g, fibre 1g, sugar none, salt 0.64g

Smoky cheese & onion tart

Cook this scrumptious large tart and cut into squares or make individual tarts.
Serve warm or cold with a crisp green salad.

TAKES ABOUT 1 HOUR ● SERVES 6

small knob of butter

6 rashers smoked bacon, chopped into pieces

3 onions, thinly sliced

200ml/7fl oz double cream

500g block shortcrust pastry (all-butter has the best flavour)

plain flour, for dusting

140g/5oz hard farmhouse cheese, such as Cheddar, half grated, half crumbled

1 egg, beaten

140g/5oz cherry tomatoes, halved

1 Heat oven to 220C/200C fan/gas 7. Heat the butter in a frying pan until sizzling, then add the bacon and cook for 6 minutes until just starting to crisp. Add the onions and sweat for 10 minutes until soft, sticky and golden. Pour in the cream, take off the heat and leave to cool a little.

2 Meanwhile, roll out the pastry on a lightly floured surface to a rectangle about 23 × 30cm and transfer to a baking sheet. Roll up the edges and press down to create a raised border.

3 Tip the creamy onions into a bowl. Mix in the grated cheese and most of the beaten egg. Spread the mixture over the pastry, then scatter over the tomatoes and crumbled cheese. Brush the borders with the remaining beaten egg, then bake for 20 minutes until golden. Leave to cool, then cut into squares.

PER SERVING 759 kcals, protein 18g, carbs 47g, fat 57g, sat fat 27g, fibre 3g, sugar 6g, salt 2.32g

Lamb cutlets al fresco

Lamb cutlets with their own little bone 'handles' are easy to eat with fingers, making them one of the best picnic meats. Serve with lots of Dijon mustard and mint jelly.

TAKES 1 HOUR ● SERVES 6

2 slices white bread
2 tbsp extra virgin olive oil
3 racks lamb, well trimmed
1 garlic clove, chopped
5 flat-leaf parsley sprigs, stalks
   discarded
5 mint sprigs, stalks discarded
2 tbsp Dijon mustard, plus extra
   to serve
mint jelly, to serve

1 Heat oven to 220C/200C fan/gas 7. Lay the bread on a baking sheet and bake for 8–10 minutes until toasted. Rub oil all over the lamb, season, then stand the racks in a roasting tin.

2 Remove the bread from the oven and roast the lamb for 10 minutes, then set aside for 5 minutes to cool. Whizz the bread, garlic, parsley, mint and some seasoning in a food processor to coarse crumbs, then tip the mixture into a wide, shallow dish.

3 When the lamb is cool, spread over the mustard. Hold a rack by the bones and sit it in the herby crumbs and press them over the mustard. Repeat with the other two racks.

4 Roast the three racks of lamb, meaty-side uppermost, for 20 minutes. If the crumbs begin to scorch, cover loosely with foil. Remove from the oven and leave until cold. Slice into cutlets and wrap in foil to transport to the picnic.

PER SERVING 276 kcals, protein 28g, carbs 6g, fat 15g, sat fat 6g, fibre none, sugar none, salt 0.77g

Garden vegetable & goat's cheese quiche

This quiche not only looks great but it really tastes of summer, with its fresh and colourful vegetables. Serve with a green salad.

TAKES 1¾ HOURS • SERVES 6

500g pack shortcrust pastry
25g/1oz plain flour, plus extra for
  dusting
50g/2oz butter
1 small courgette, topped, tailed and
  sliced
85g/3oz runner beans, stringed, halved
  lengthways and sliced
85g/3oz fresh or thawed frozen peas
3 salad onions, stems chopped and
  bulbs quartered
300ml/½ pint milk
2 eggs
100g log full-fat soft goat's cheese,
  sliced
3 small vine tomatoes, quartered

1 Heat oven to 220C/200C fan/gas 7. Roll out the pastry on a lightly floured surface and line a deep, 24cm-round, loose-bottomed flan tin. Prick the pastry with a fork then chill for 20 minutes. Cover with baking parchment and baking beans, and bake for 10 minutes. Remove the parchment and beans then bake for 5 minutes more until crisp.

2 Turn oven down to 190C/170C fan/ gas 5. Melt the butter in a medium pan and cook the green vegetables and onions for 5 minutes, until starting to soften. Tip the milk and flour into the pan and stir over the heat until it thickens to a smooth sauce. Cool for 5 minutes, stirring to stop a skin forming.

3 Beat the eggs into the sauce and generously season. Pour into the pastry case and scatter with goat's cheese and tomatoes. Bake for 40 minutes until the filling is set and turning golden. Serve warm or cold.

PER SERVING 449 kcals, protein 15g, carbs 35g, fat 29g, sat fat 17g, fibre 3g, sugar none, salt 0.96g

Scotch egg pasties

These pasties have all the flavour of Scotch eggs, but are a lot easier to make as there is no deep-frying involved. Serve with piccalilli or brown sauce.

TAKES 1 HOUR 10 MINUTES

● **MAKES 8**

9 medium eggs (it's important they're not large)

8 good-quality large pork sausages, meat squeezed out

6 spring onions, finely sliced

2 × 500g blocks frozen shortcrust pastry, defrosted

plain flour, for dusting

1 Lower eight of the eggs into a pan of boiling water. Bring back to the boil and simmer for 6 minutes. Drain, then cool under cold water. Peel carefully. Mix the sausagemeat and onions together.

2 Roll out each block of pastry until large enough to cut out 3 × 18cm circles. Re-roll the trimmings; you should get four circles from each block. Have two baking sheets ready, dusted with flour.

3 Using damp hands, squash out one-eighth of the sausage mix over each pastry round, going almost right to the edges. Dampen the edges of the pastry. Sit an egg in the middle of the sausagemeat, season, then pull the sides up over egg and seal. Crimp the edges and put on to the baking sheets.

4 Beat the final egg and brush over the pasties. Chill for 30 minutes. Heat oven to 220C/200C fan/gas 7. Bake the pasties, one sheet at a time, for 25 minutes until golden, then leave to cool.

PER PASTY 795 kcals, protein 22g, carbs 63g, fat 52g, sat fat 19g, fibre 3g, sugar 2g, salt 2.19g

Savoury baked ricotta

This traditional Italian dish is delicious cold or warm. To carry to a picnic, enclose the dish completely in a double thickness of foil and seal well.

TAKES 1 HOUR • SERVES 4

25g/1oz unsalted butter
50g/2oz Parmesan, grated
300g/10oz cherry tomatoes
1 garlic clove, cut in half
1 tbsp extra virgin olive oil, plus extra
    for drizzling
6 eggs
500g tub ricotta
200ml tub crème fraîche
2 tbsp fresh thyme leaves

1 Heat oven to 200C/180C fan/gas 6. Butter an ovenproof baking dish, approximately 36 × 24cm, and sprinkle with the grated Parmesan. Toss the tomatoes with the garlic and oil, and season. Tip on to a baking sheet and cook for 15 minutes, until softened.

2 Mix the eggs and ricotta in a food processor until blended. Put in a bowl and stir in the crème fraîche and half the thyme. Season.

3 Spoon the ricotta mixture into the baking dish, scatter with the tomatoes and remaining thyme. Drizzle with oil and bake for 20 minutes until set.

PER SERVING 446 kcals, protein 20g, carbs 4g, fat 39g, sat fat 20g, fibre 1g, sugar none, salt 0.62g

Smoked salmon, dill & onion tart

Cook the flaky pastry case the day before and top with soft onions, smoked salmon and lemony crème fraîche the next day to make this stunning tart.

TAKES 1¼ HOURS • SERVES 6

plain flour, for dusting
375g pack puff pastry
1 medium red onion, thinly sliced into rings
1 tbsp olive oil
zest 1 lemon, plus juice ½ lemon
5 tbsp crème fraîche, plus extra for drizzling
200g/7oz smoked salmon, sliced into pieces
2 tsp capers, drained
20g pack dill, chopped

1 Heat oven to 200C/180C fan/gas 6. On a floured board, roll out the pastry to the thickness of a £1 coin. Press into a 20cm tart tin with a removable base. Line with baking paper and fill with baking beans. Bake for 20–25 minutes until the pastry turns golden. Remove the beans and paper, and prick all over with a fork. Cook the tart for another 10 minutes until the pastry is biscuity brown all over. Leave the pastry case to cool on a wire rack.

2 Cook the onion in a pan in the oil for 5 minutes until soft. Season and set aside to cool. Stir together the lemon juice and crème fraîche, then set aside.

3 Spread the onion in the tart and arrange the salmon on top. Sprinkle over the capers, dill and lemon zest. Cover with cling film or foil and chill. Serve drizzled with the lemony crème fraîche.

PER SERVING 381 kcals, protein 11g, carbs 29g, fat 25g, sat fat 10g, fibre 1g, sugar none, salt 0.68g

Cheesy spinach bake

This crisp filo pastry bake can be sliced into portions to serve. For a change, you could add a layer of ham. Serve with some hot chilli sauce.

TAKES 1 HOUR • SERVES 8

200g pack feta
2 × 250g tubs ricotta
3 × 100g bags baby leaf spinach,
  chopped
1 bunch spring onions, finely sliced
50g/2oz Parmesan, grated
1 egg, beaten
good grating nutmeg
100g/3½oz breadcrumbs
2 tbsp olive oil
6 sheets filo pastry

1 Heat oven to 180C/160C fan/gas 4. Mash the feta in a large mixing bowl, add the ricotta and mash again thoroughly to mix. Stir in the spinach, spring onions, Parmesan, egg, nutmeg and plenty of seasoning with half the breadcrumbs.
2 Brush a 20 × 30cm tin with a little oil. Layer in half the filo sheets, brushing each with oil before adding the next. Scatter the remaining breadcrumbs evenly over the base. Spoon in the ricotta filling and gently spread so as not to dislodge the breadcrumbs. Cover with the remaining filo, brushing with oil as you go, then score into eight portions. Bake for 35–40 minutes until golden and crisp. Eat warm or cold.

PER SERVING 436 kcals, protein 23g, carbs 32g, fat 25g, sat fat 13g, fibre 2g, sugar 5g, salt 2g

Poached beef fillet with watercress & walnut salad

Poaching is the perfect method for cooking small joints of meat in summer. Slice the meat and pack separately with the salad and dressing for a picnic or lunch.

TAKES 45 MINUTES • SERVES 4

1 litre/1¾ pints stock (from a cube is fine), plus 2 extra tbsp
1 large onion, sliced
1 fennel bulb, sliced
1 large carrot, sliced
2 bay leaves and 2 rosemary sprigs
500g/1lb 2oz joint beef fillet
sea salt flakes

FOR THE SALAD

100g bag watercress
4 tbsp extra virgin olive oil
1 tbsp balsamic vinegar
1 tsp Dijon mustard
50g/2oz chopped walnuts

1 Put the stock on to boil with the onion, fennel, carrot and herbs. Cover and simmer for 10 minutes. Trim the beef fillet of any sinew – do not tie it.

2 Season the beef all over, then lower into the simmering stock. Allow the stock to return to a gentle boil, then lower the heat until it is barely simmering. Cover, then cook for 18 minutes for medium–rare, 22 minutes for well done. Remove the pan from the heat, leave the meat to stand for 15 minutes in the stock, remove and pat dry. Slice into eight.

3 Make the salad by scattering the watercress leaves over a small serving plate. Whisk together the oil, vinegar, mustard and some seasoning. Drizzle half over the leaves and scatter with the nuts. Arrange the meat on top and mix the 2 tablespoons of the stock with the remaining dressing. Pour over the beef, sprinkle with sea salt flakes and serve with new potatoes.

PER SERVING 368 kcals, protein 29g, carbs 1g, fat 28g, sat fat 6g, fibre 1g, sugar none, salt 0.51g

Goat's cheese, potato & onion tart

The perfect tart – easy to make, looks stunning and tastes wonderful, and it can be tucked away in the freezer for up to a month.

TAKES 1 HOUR ● SERVES 6

250g/9oz pack shortcrust pastry, fresh or frozen
25g/1oz butter
1 tbsp olive oil
2 onions, sliced
1 medium potato, peeled and sliced
2 garlic cloves, crushed
2 tbsp fresh thyme leaves
140g/5oz goat's cheese, broken into small pieces
3 eggs
200ml tub crème fraîche, half-fat is fine
100g bag rocket leaves, to garnish

1 Heat oven to 190C/170C fan/gas 5. Roll out the pastry to fit a deep, 23cm-round, loose-bottomed tart tin, then line the tin with the pastry. Chill for 30 minutes. Line the pastry with baking parchment, fill with baking beans, and bake for 15 minutes. Remove the parchment and beans and return the tart to the oven for 5 minutes until golden, then remove and set aside. Reduce oven to 180C/160C fan/gas 4.

2 Heat the butter and oil in a frying pan, add the onions and potato, and cook over a very gentle heat for 10–15 minutes until golden. Season, then add the garlic and thyme, and cook for a further 3 minutes. Tip into the pastry case with the goat's cheese and spread out evenly.

3 Whisk together the eggs and crème fraîche, season, then pour into the pastry case and bake for 30–35 minutes until golden brown and set in the centre. Scatter over the rocket leaves and serve.

PER SERVING 502 kcals, protein 12g, carbs 25g, fat 40g, sat fat 21g, fibre 2g, sugar none, salt 0.08g

Creamy potato salad with broad beans

Homemade potato salad is so much tastier than shop-bought. Charlotte potatoes, with their dense flesh and nutty flavour, are good for this low-fat recipe.

TAKES 35 MINUTES • SERVES 4

200g/7oz broad beans, fresh and podded, or frozen
750g/1lb 10oz salad or new potatoes
1 red onion, very thinly sliced
2 tbsp white wine vinegar
½ tsp sugar
150ml pot soured cream
bunch chives, snipped
½ tsp Dijon mustard

1 Heat a pan of salted water and, once boiling, add the broad beans. Bring the pan back to the boil for 2 minutes, then lift the beans out with a slotted spoon into a bowl of cold water. Tip the potatoes into the pan, then boil for 15–20 minutes or until tender. Drain, and leave to cool. While the potatoes are cooking, put the onion into a shallow bowl, splash with the vinegar and scatter over the sugar, then leave to soak. Pop the beans out of their jackets.

2 For the dressing, mix the soured cream, chives, mustard, 1 tablespoon water and plenty of seasoning. Measure 2 teaspoons of the vinegary juices from the onion, then stir into the dressing to combine. Taste and add more of the vinegar, if you like, then discard the rest. Peel the potatoes, if you prefer, then cut them in half and toss with the dressing, onions and beans.

PER SERVING 251 kcals, protein 8g, carbs 38g, fat 9g, sat fat 5g, fibre 5g, sugar 7g, salt 0.15g

Red cabbage & fennel coleslaw

This health-packed crunchy salad travels well. It's low in fat, a good source of vitamin C and counts as one of your 5-a-day.

TAKES 15 MINUTES ● SERVES 4

½ small red cabbage, shredded

2 medium carrots, coarsely grated

1 fennel bulb, cut into quarters and shredded

2 shallots, thinly sliced

50g/2oz mayonnaise

1 Put the cabbage, carrots, fennel and shallots in a large bowl and toss together until thoroughly mixed.

2 Stir in the mayonnaise to coat the salad, then season with lots of freshly ground black pepper and a little salt. Any leftovers can be stored in a sealed container in the fridge for up to 2 days.

PER SERVING 117 kcals, protein 1g, carbs 6g, fat 10g, sat fat 2g, fibre 3g, sugar 6g, salt 0.19g

Indian summer salad

This low-fat salad makes a great alternative to coleslaw and is lighter, fresher tasting and more colourful.

TAKES 20 MINUTES • SERVES 6

3 carrots
bunch radishes
2 courgettes
½ small red onion
small handful mint leaves, roughly torn

FOR THE DRESSING

1 tbsp white wine vinegar
1 tsp Dijon mustard
1 tbsp mayonnaise
2 tbsp olive oil

1 Grate the carrots into a large bowl. Thinly slice the radishes and courgettes, and finely chop the onion. Mix all the vegetables together in the bowl with the mint leaves.

2 Whisk together the vinegar, mustard and mayonnaise until smooth, then gradually whisk in the oil. Taste and add salt and pepper, then drizzle over the salad and mix well. (Leftovers will keep in a covered container in the fridge for up to 24 hours.)

PER SERVING 79 kcals, protein 1g, carbs 5g, fat 6g, sat fat 1g, fibre 2g, sugar 6g, salt 0.35g

Green beans & mushrooms with tangy soy dressing

Forget limp salad leaves, here's a dress-ahead salad that retains its good looks. You can prepare it the day before and keep it chilled.

TAKES 15–20 MINUTES • SERVES 6

300g/10oz French green beans, trimmed
100g/3½oz small white mushrooms, halved
20g pack chives, snipped
5 tbsp soy sauce
1 tbsp grated fresh root ginger
1 tbsp clear honey
1 garlic clove, crushed with a knife
2 tbsp lemon juice
5 tbsp extra virgin olive oil

1 Boil the beans in salted water for 5–7 minutes, then drain and submerge in a bowl of iced water. Pat dry with a tea towel and tip into a bowl with the mushrooms and chives.

2 Put the rest of the ingredients into a small jar and shake well. Pour over the beans and toss gently. Pack in a covered container and chill.

PER SERVING 112 kcals, protein 2g, carbs 5g, fat 10g, sat fat 1g, fibre 1g, sugar 2g, salt 2.26g

Layered houmous, tabbouleh & feta picnic bowl

The tabbouleh, a salad of herbs mixed with bulghar wheat, is dressed but won't spoil if you make it ahead, and because the lettuce is packed on top, it won't go soggy.

TAKES 35 MINUTES ● SERVES 4

2 × 200g tubs houmous
400g can chickpeas, drained and rinsed
200g pack feta, broken into chunks
handful pitted black olives
1 crisp romaine lettuce heart
flatbreads, to serve

FOR THE TABBOULEH

85g/3oz bulghar wheat
80g bunch mint, leaves finely chopped
80g bunch flat-leaf parsley, leaves
  finely chopped
2 large ripe tomatoes, deseeded and
  chopped
1 red onion, finely chopped
zest and juice 1 lemon
4 tbsp olive oil, plus extra for drizzling

1 Tip the bulghar into a pan, cover with water, season with salt, then bring to the boil and simmer for 15 minutes until tender. Drain in a sieve, rinse under cold water, then leave to drain over the pan. Mix the mint and parsley with the tomatoes, onion and drained bulghar. Whisk the lemon zest, juice, oil and some seasoning, then toss this through.

2 Spoon the houmous into a portable picnic bowl. Scatter with chickpeas, then sprinkle with seasoning and drizzle with a little of the extra oil. Spoon the tabbouleh on top. Top with the feta and olives, then tear over the lettuce leaves.

3 Cover the bowl tightly. Put a little more oil in a container to take with you, then chill the salad for up to 24 hours.

4 To eat, drizzle with oil, then scoop on to serving plates. Serve with some flatbreads alongside.

PER SERVING 768 kcals, protein 24g, carbs 41g, fat 58g, sat fat 13g, fibre 9g, sugar 7g, salt 2.85g

Roast tomato salad

Ripe summer tomatoes are perfect for this recipe and are packed with vitamin C. A perfect side dish to tarts and flans.

TAKES 10 MINUTES ● SERVES 4

500g/1lb 2oz cherry tomatoes
2 garlic cloves
2 tbsp olive oil
several thyme sprigs

1 Heat oven to 180C/160C fan/gas 4. Put the whole cherry tomatoes, garlic, oil and several thyme sprigs into a small roasting tin.

2 Add some seasoning and mix together. Roast for 5–8 minutes and cool. Pack into a rigid plastic container with a tight-fitting lid to carry to a picnic.

PER SERVING 75 kcals, protein 1g, carbs 4g, fat 6g, sat fat 1g, fibre 1g, sugar none, salt 0.04g

Tangy carrot, red cabbage & onion salad

Crunchy textures and punchy flavours combine in this modern-style salad. It counts as two of your 5-a-day and is a good source of vitamin C.

TAKES 15 MINUTES ● SERVES 4

4 carrots, cut into thin sticks or grated
½ red cabbage, finely shredded
2 small red onions, finely sliced
handful mint leaves
handful coriander leaves
handful toasted peanuts, roughly
    chopped

FOR THE DRESSING

juice 2 limes
1 tbsp groundnut oil
1 red chilli, deseeded and finely
    chopped
1 tbsp soft brown sugar

1 Tip the carrots, cabbage and onions into a bowl. Make the dressing by stirring the ingredients together until the sugar has dissolved.

2 Pour over the salad, tossing the vegetables in the dressing. Add the herbs, toss again, then scatter over the peanuts.

PER SERVING 146 kcals, protein 4g, carbs 17g, fat 7g, sat fat 1g, fibre 5g, sugar 15g, salt 0.08g

Minted potato salad

Using yogurt instead of mayonnaise makes a low-fat version of this favourite.
The fresh mix of flavours is just the thing for eating out on a summer's day.

TAKES 25 MINUTES • SERVES 6

1kg/2lb 4oz small new potatoes
1 garlic clove, crushed
200g/7oz natural yogurt
1 tsp white wine vinegar
1 tsp caster sugar
3 spring onions, finely sliced
large handful mint leaves, roughly torn

1 Boil the potatoes in a pan of water for 15 minutes or until tender, then drain and cool.

2 Stir together the garlic, yogurt, vinegar and sugar with some seasoning to make the dressing. To serve, mix most of the spring onions and mint into the dressing, then pour it over the potatoes. Stir gently, taking care not to break up the potatoes. Scatter with the rest of the spring onions and mint to serve.

PER SERVING 140 kcals, protein 5g, carbs 30g, fat 1g, sat fat none, fibre 2g, sugar 5g, salt 0.11g

Thai cucumber salad with sour chilli dressing

If you're transporting this, keep the leaves crisp by putting the veg and dressing in separate containers. This salad is packed with vitamin C and is low in fat too.

TAKES 10 MINUTES • SERVES 4

1 cucumber, cut into ribbons with
   a peeler
1 Little Gem lettuce, shredded
140g/5oz beansprouts
bunch coriander, leaves roughly
   chopped
bunch mint, leaves roughly chopped

FOR THE DRESSING

1 tsp rice wine vinegar
1 tbsp fish sauce
½ tsp light muscovado sugar
2 red chillies, deseeded and finely
   chopped

1 Mix the dressing ingredients together, stirring until the sugar is dissolved.
2 Put the salad ingredients in a bowl, then pour over the dressing, mixing well to combine. Serve immediately.

PER SERVING 27 kcals, protein 2g, carbs 4g, fat 1g, sat fat none, fibre 1g, sugar 3g, salt 0.75g

Mexican bean salad

Eat this salad as it is or pile it into the centre of a flour tortilla, then grate over some Cheddar and add a dollop of yogurt. Roll up the tortilla to serve.

TAKES 20 MINUTES ● SERVES 4

4 eggs

2 avocados, peeled and stoned

2 × 400g cans beans (we used kidney beans and pinto beans), drained and rinsed

1 small red onion, finely sliced

large bunch coriander, leaves only, roughly chopped

250g punnet cherry tomatoes, halved

3 tbsp good-quality dressing of your choice

1 red chilli, deseeded and finely sliced

½ tsp ground cumin

1 Lower the eggs into boiling water and boil for 6½ minutes, then put into a bowl of cold water to cool. Slice the avocados and put in a large bowl with the beans, onion, coriander and tomatoes. Spoon the dressing into a small bowl, then mix in the chilli and cumin.

2 Once the eggs have cooled, peel off the shells and cut into quarters. Toss the salad with the dressing and nestle in the eggs.

PER SERVING 430 kcals, protein 20g, carbs 25g, fat 29g, sat fat 3g, fibre 10g, sugar 6g, salt 1.61g

Big egg, bacon & bean salad

A substantial 'almost-niçoise' salad that won't get soggy in transit. It's good served all summer long with chunks of Brie and crispy fresh baguettes.

TAKES 30 MINUTES • SERVES 6

750g/1lb 10oz salad potatoes
3 eggs
200g/7oz fine green beans, trimmed
6 rashers smoked streaky or back
  bacon
100g/3½oz Kalamata olives, stones in
  or out, it's up to you
100g bag baby leaf spinach
handful shop-bought croutons, to
  garnish

FOR THE DRESSING

1 garlic clove, crushed
3 tbsp olive oil
1 tbsp white wine, red wine or cider
  vinegar
1 tsp Dijon mustard
2 tsp capers, drained
2 anchovy fillets, finely chopped
  (optional)

1 Bring a large pan of water to the boil, then drop in the potatoes and set the timer for 20 minutes. With 8 minutes to go, add the eggs to the pan, making sure they're submerged. With 4 minutes to go, add the green beans. When the cooking time is up, drain everything in a colander, then cool under cold water.

2 Heat grill to high. Grill the bacon for about 8 minutes until crisp and golden. Snip into bite-size pieces. Whisk the dressing ingredients together with some seasoning and pour into an airtight container. Peel the eggs and cut the potatoes in half. Layer up the potatoes, beans, olives, spinach and bacon in a large lidded container, then tuck the eggs around. Chill.

3 Just before eating, lift out the eggs and halve them. Whisk the dressing again, then toss the salad with most of the dressing. Scatter the eggs and croutons on top, drizzle over the remaining dressing, then tuck in.

PER SERVING 303 kcals, protein 11g, carbs 26g, fat 18g, sat fat 4g, fibre 3g, sugar 3g, salt 1.85g

Tuna pasta salad

Made in just 20 minutes, this tasty salad can be eaten warm or cold. Why not serve it for supper and then take the leftovers to work for lunch the next day?

TAKES 20 MINUTES • SERVES 4

300g/10oz penne
4 tbsp mayonnaise
juice ½ lemon
200g can tuna in olive oil
2 red peppers, deseeded and thinly
   sliced
1 red onion, halved and finely sliced
large handful rocket leaves, to garnish

1 Cook the pasta according to the pack instructions. Meanwhile, tip the mayonnaise, lemon juice and 1 tablespoon of the tuna oil into a large bowl and mix. Drain the rest of the oil from the tuna, then flake the fish into the bowl and mix well.

2 Drain the pasta and toss it with the mayonnaise mixture, peppers and onion. Scatter over the rocket just before serving the salad.

PER SERVING 476 kcals, protein 21g, carbs 64g, fat 17g, sat fat 3g, fibre 4g, sugar 8g, salt 0.5g

Green bean, olive & anchovy salad

The anchovies melt into the olive oil and will have given the beans a gutsy flavour by the time you're ready to eat.

TAKES 20 MINUTES • SERVES 4

500g/1lb 2oz green beans
4 tbsp extra virgin olive oil
10 salted anchovy fillets, rinsed and dried
25g/1oz capers
juice 1 lemon
100g/3½oz niçoise olives
small handful basil leaves

1 Cook the beans in a pan of salted boiling water until soft, probably around 3 minutes. Drain, season and toss with 2 tablespoons of the oil. Chop the anchovies and capers together, put into a bowl, and stir in lemon juice to combine. Add the remaining oil and stir.

2 Pit the olives and tear the basil. Mix the beans into the sauce. Scatter with the olives and basil. Put the salad in a rigid container with a tight-fitting lid, if you're taking it to a picnic.

PER SERVING 171 kcals, protein 5g, carbs 4g, fat 15g, sat fat 2g, fibre 4g, sugar none, salt 2.70g

Summer potato salad with minty Dijon mayo

Everyone loves potato salad – and this recipe, packed with veg, has more to offer than usual, in both flavour and glamour.

TAKES 30–40 MINUTES • SERVES 8

FOR THE DRESSING

300ml/½ pint mayonnaise
2 rounded tbsp Dijon mustard
2 tbsp chopped fresh mint

FOR THE SALAD

750g pack baby Jersey royals
400g/14oz fine green beans, trimmed
450g/1lb frozen peas, thawed
2 large ripe avocados
juice ½ lemon

1 Mix all the dressing ingredients with a little salt and pepper and 2 tablespoons water until well blended. Halve or thickly slice the potatoes, if large, then boil for 7–8 minutes in a pan of salted water with a steamer full of beans over the top until they are both tender. Cool them separately under the cold tap.

2 Pile the potatoes into a bowl followed by the beans and peas. Just before serving, peel, stone and chop the avocados, and toss with the lemon juice to stop them discolouring. Pile on top of the salad and drizzle over the dressing. Cover the bowl with cling film to transport. Toss just before serving to coat everything in the mayo dressing.

PER SERVING 457 kcals, protein 8g, carbs 25g, fat 37g, sat fat 6g, fibre 6g, sugar none, salt 0.83g

Asian beef salad

This zesty, low-fat salad can be packed up for a picnic or makes a great speedy supper dish for a summer evening.

TAKES 25 MINUTES • SERVES 4

250g pack rice noodles

4 tbsp soy sauce

juice 1 lime

thumb-sized piece of ginger, peeled and grated

2 tbsp olive oil

200g/7oz sliced roast beef from the deli counter

1 red pepper, deseeded and sliced

½ cucumber, sliced

handful coriander leaves, chopped

1 Soak the rice noodles according to the pack instructions. Whisk together the soy sauce, lime juice, ginger and oil in a large serving bowl. Drain the noodles well, then tip into the bowl.

2 Cut the beef into bite-size pieces then add to the bowl along with the remaining ingredients. Toss everything together.

PER SERVING 377 kcals, protein 20g, carbs 59g, fat 9g, sat fat 2g, fibre 2g, sugar 4g, salt 2.80g

Help-yourself tuna rice salad

This hearty salad is ideal for busy households. It keeps well in the fridge for up to 3 days and can be spooned into a bowl or lunchbox.

TAKES 30 MINUTES ● SERVES 8

approx 900g/2lb cold cooked rice
   (about 400g/14oz uncooked rice)
2 × 200g cans tuna in spring water,
   drained
200g/7oz frozen petits pois, defrosted
   under the hot tap
2 red peppers, deseeded and diced
3 tomatoes, chopped into small chunks
5 spring onions, finely sliced
bunch flat-leaf parsley, chopped
large handful pitted green olives,
   roughly chopped (optional)
4 tbsp mayonnaise
juice 1 lemon
2 tbsp extra virgin olive oil

1 The cooked rice will probably have clumped together, so break it up in a large mixing bowl. Flake in the tuna, then mix in the peas, peppers, tomatoes, spring onions, parsley and olives, if you're using them.

2 Stir through the mayonnaise, lemon juice and oil, and season to taste. Cover the bowl with cling film or put in a large plastic container and let your family serve themselves whenever they are hungry, or use it to fill up their lunchboxes.

PER SERVING 328 kcals, protein 14g, carbs 49g, fat 10g, sat fat 2g, fibre 2g, sugar 5g, salt 0.22g

Best-ever crab sandwiches

Fresh crab sandwiches conjure up thoughts of a summer day at the seaside and couldn't be easier or taste more delicious than in this updated, deep-filled recipe.

TAKES 20 MINUTES • MAKES 4

8 hand-cut slices best-quality brown or
  granary bread
unsalted butter, for spreading
1 lemon, cut into 4 wedges, to garnish

FOR THE CRAB PASTE

brown crabmeat from 1 large brown
  crab, about 1.5kg/3lb 5oz in its shell
  (reserve the white meat, see below)
1 tbsp mayonnaise
1 tsp tomato ketchup
juice ½ lemon
1 tsp Dijon mustard
big pinch cayenne pepper
few drops brandy (optional)

FOR THE WHITE MEAT

picked white meat from the same crab
small handful chopped mixed herbs,
  such as parsley, dill, tarragon, chervil
  and chives
juice ½ lemon
2 tbsp olive oil

1 Make the crab paste: mix the ingredients together in a bowl and season, then set aside. In a separate bowl, mix the white meat with the herbs, lemon juice, oil and a little seasoning to taste.

2 Spread the bread lightly with butter, then spoon and spread the crab paste over four of the slices. Pile the white meat over, then top with the remaining bread. Cut the crusts off, if you like, and serve halved or in small triangles or squares with lemon wedges on the side.

PER SANDWICH 529 kcals, protein 30g, carbs 41g, fat 28g, sat fat 9g, fibre 3g, sugar 3g, salt 2.65g

Borlotti bean salad with prawns, rocket & mozzarella

Borlotti – brown beans from Italy – are very similar to cannellini, with the same oval shape and creamy texture.

TAKES 10–15 MINUTES ● SERVES 6

400g can borlotti beans, drained and rinsed

1 ball mozzarella, drained and cut in chunks

200g/7oz cooked king prawns, peeled

1 small red onion, thinly sliced into half moons

225g pack cherry tomatoes, halved

100g bag rocket leaves

FOR THE DRESSING

1 anchovy, rinsed and finely chopped

10 capers, rinsed and chopped

1 garlic clove, finely chopped

2 tbsp red wine vinegar

6 tbsp extra virgin olive oil

1 Put the beans, mozzarella, prawns, onion and tomatoes into a container.

2 Add the dressing ingredients to a small jar and shake well to mix. Pour the dressing over the salad, then refrigerate until taking to the picnic. Just before serving, toss the rocket leaves through.

PER SERVING 294 kcals, protein 19g, carbs 9g, fat 20g, sat fat 7g, fibre 3g, sugar none, salt 2.1g

10-minute couscous salad

This makes a great lunchbox filler for a day out and is equally good at home straight from the fridge. It's easily doubled to serve more.

TAKES 10 MINUTES ● SERVES 2

100g/3½oz couscous

200ml/7fl oz hot low-salt vegetable stock (from a cube is fine)

2 spring onions

1 red pepper

½ cucumber

2 tbsp pesto

50g/2oz feta, cubed

2 tbsp toasted pine nuts

1 Tip the couscous into a large bowl and pour over the hot stock. Cover, then leave for 10 minutes, until fluffy and all the stock has been absorbed.

2 Slice the onions and pepper, and dice the cucumber. Add these to the couscous. Fork through the pesto and crumble in the feta. Sprinkle over the pine nuts to serve.

PER SERVING 327 kcals, protein 13g, carbs 33g, fat 17g, sat fat 5g, fibre 2g, sugar 7g, salt 0.88g

Prosciutto & fig salad

Using top-quality ingredients turns this simple dish into something altogether more special. Pack ingredients separately and assemble at the picnic.

TAKES 10 MINUTES ● SERVES 4

juice 1 lemon
4–6 tbsp extra virgin olive oil
9 ripe black or green figs, split
1 bunch young mint, leaves picked
1 bunch purple or green basil, leaves
   picked
100g bag rocket leaves
12 slices prosciutto crudo di San
   Daniele

1 Make a dressing by mixing the lemon juice with the oil, and season generously.
2 Toss the figs with the herbs and rocket leaves and the dressing. Put on individual plates, combining the ham slices into the salad as you do so.

PER SERVING 157 kcals, protein 14g, carbs 13g, fat 6g, sat fat 2g, fibre 2g, sugar none, salt 2.15g

Mediterranean-style bean salad

The creamy goat's cheese is nicely offset by the salty Kalamata olives. For a change, add a can of flaked tuna to the salad instead of the cheese.

TAKES 10 MINUTES • SERVES 4

290g jar artichoke hearts in oil
1 tbsp sun-dried tomato paste
1 tsp white wine vinegar
410g can cannellini beans, drained
    and rinsed
300g pack small vine tomatoes,
    quartered (about 12 in total)
handful Kalamata olives
2 spring onions, thinly sliced on
    the diagonal
200g log soft goat's cheese, crumbled

1 Drain the jar of artichokes, reserving 3 tablespoons of the oil. Pour the oil into a bowl, stir in the sun-dried tomato paste and vinegar and mix until smooth. Season to taste.

2 Roughly chop the artichokes and tip into a large bowl with the cannellini beans, tomatoes, olives, spring onions and half the goat's cheese. Stir in the artichoke-oil mixture and tip into a serving bowl. Season to taste. Crumble over the remaining goat's cheese, then serve.

PER SERVING 367 kcals, protein 13g, carbs 16g, fat 28g, sat fat 7g, fibre 6g, sugar none, salt 3g

Crunchy Asian cabbage & prawn salad

This easy-to-put-together crunchy mix of veg and peanuts is tossed with a delicious Asian-flavoured dressing – a superb combination. Keep the dish chilled in transit.

TAKES 20 MINUTES • SERVES 4–6

250g/9oz Chinese cabbage
175g/6oz white cabbage
2 celery sticks
2 carrots
small handful mint leaves, chopped
small handful coriander leaves,
   chopped
200g/7oz large cooked peeled prawns
4 tbsp roasted peanuts, chopped

FOR THE DRESSING

1–2 small red chillies, sliced
1 garlic clove, crushed
2 tbsp caster sugar
2 tbsp rice vinegar
3 tbsp lime juice
3 tbsp fish sauce

1 Shred the cabbages, celery and carrots finely on a mandolin or grate them on the largest holes of a grater. Add the mint and coriander to the vegetables along with the prawns. Toss everything together.

2 Make the dressing by whisking all the ingredients together. Dress the salad, tip it into a bowl, sprinkle over the peanuts and serve.

PER SERVING (4) 198 kcals, protein 18g, carbs 18g, fat 7g, sat fat 1g, fibre 4g, sugar 16g, salt 3.18g

No-bake bean spread

Spoon this quick and easy spread into pitta breads with cucumber sticks and tomato or spread on a wrap and fill with sliced red pepper and shredded lettuce.

TAKES 10 MINUTES • SERVES 6

410g can butter beans, drained and
 rinsed
2 tbsp olive oil
2 tbsp lemon juice
125g packet light garlic and herb
 cheese

1 Put the butter beans into a food processor, then pour in the oil and lemon juice. Add a pinch of salt and some freshly ground black pepper. Whizz together to make a smooth paste.
2 Add the garlic and herb cheese, blend until smooth, then put into a sealable container and chill. (This spread will keep in the refrigerator for up to 3 days.)

PER SERVING 102 kcals, protein 4g, carbs 6g, fat 7g, sat fat 2g, fibre 2g, sugar 1g, salt 0.57g

Storecupboard pasta salad

This low-fat, filling salad is perfect for kids' lunchboxes and can easily be doubled.
To ring the changes, stir through some sweetcorn and a little mayo.

TAKES 5 MINUTES ● SERVES 2

2 tsp finely chopped red onion

1 tsp capers

1 tbsp pesto

2 tsp olive oil

185g can tuna in spring water, drained

100g/3½oz leftover cooked pasta
    shapes

3 sun-dried tomatoes, chopped

1 Mix together the chopped onion, capers, pesto and oil.

2 Flake the tuna into a bowl with the pasta and tomatoes, then stir in the pesto mix. (Can be made the night before.)

PER SERVING 189 kcals, protein 19g, carbs 12g, fat 7g, sat fat 2g, fibre 2g, sugar 2g, salt 0.91g

Ploughman's lunchbox

Get the children to put together their own favourite version of this classic. Pear and a blue cheese work well, or add some grapes, dates or dried apricots.

TAKES 10 MINUTES ● SERVES 1

1 apple
lemon juice
2 Baby Gem lettuce leaves
2 tbsp chutney
1 small carrot, grated
3 cherry tomatoes
1 tbsp mustard cress
1 chunk Cheddar
crackers, to serve

1 Cut the apple into chunks, remove the core, and squeeze over the lemon juice to prevent the apple going brown.
2 Put the Baby Gem leaves in a container, then spoon the chutney into one leaf. Mix together the carrot, tomatoes and cress, and put on the other salad leaf. Add the apple chunks and Cheddar, and serve with a selection of crackers.

PER SERVING 463 kcals, protein 16g, carbs 59g, fat 20g, sat fat 10g, fibre 6g, sugar 29g, salt 1.8g

Tomato & mozzarella couscous salad

This is simple enough for children to make themselves for an after-school snack or a packed lunch to take to school.

TAKES 10–15 MINUTES • SERVES 4

1 teacup (about 225g/8oz) couscous
1 tbsp pesto (red or green will be fine)
½ vegetable stock cube
150g pack mozzarella, torn into pieces
2 large tomatoes, chopped
handful rocket or other salad leaves

FOR THE DRESSING

4 tbsp olive oil
1 tbsp pesto (red or green)
juice 1 lemon

1 Tip the couscous into a large bowl along with the pesto and crumble over the stock cube. Pour over 2 teacups (about 400ml/14fl oz) boiling water and give it a good stir to dissolve the stock. Cover with cling film and leave to stand for 10 minutes until all the water has been absorbed.

2 To make the dressing, mix together the oil, pesto and lemon juice. When the couscous has swelled up, pour the dressing over and flake through with a fork, breaking up any clumps. Toss in the mozzarella and tomatoes, garnish with rocket, then serve.

PER SERVING 363 kcals, protein 13g, carbs 32g, fat 22g, sat fat 7g, fibre 1g, sugar none, salt 1.02g

Beet, spinach & goat's cheese couscous

Put together this easy lunchbox salad the night before and you'll find the flavours are even better the next day. This recipe is easily doubled.

TAKES 10 MINUTES ● SERVES 2

zest and juice 1 large orange
140g/5oz couscous
25g/1oz walnut pieces
85g/3oz firm goat's cheese, crumbled
6 dried apricots, roughly chopped
4 small cooked beetroot, quartered
2 handfuls spinach leaves

FOR THE DRESSING

2 tbsp extra virgin olive oil
juice ½ lemon

1 Put the orange zest, juice and 100ml/3½fl oz water in a small pan and bring to the boil. Put the couscous in a medium bowl and pour the hot liquid over. Mix well, then cover and leave to absorb for 5 minutes.

2 Fluff up the couscous grains with a fork, then add the walnuts, cheese, apricots, beetroot and some seasoning. Mix the oil and lemon juice (or use your favourite shop-bought vinaigrette), then toss the dressing into the couscous. Pack separately in two sealed containers, with the spinach sat on top (it won't go soggy when layered up this way). When ready to eat, toss the spinach through.

PER SERVING 601 kcals, protein 21g, carbs 57g, fat 34g, sat fat 11g, fibre 5g, sugar 22g, salt 1.13g

Greek lamb baguette

Here's a great idea for using up the Sunday roast and it's easily doubled or tripled. Wrap the filled baguettes tightly in cling film to carry to work.

TAKES 5 MINUTES • SERVES 1

1 small baguette, cut lengthways
sprinkle olive oil and red wine vinegar
pinch dried oregano
handful leftover lamb
few slices red pepper and red or white onion
shredded lettuce
3 tbsp crumbled feta

1 Sprinkle the inside of the baguette with a little oil, vinegar, oregano and a little seasoning.
2 Layer the lamb, red pepper, onion, lettuce and feta into the baguette, then wrap tightly in cling film.

PER BAGUETTE 762 kcals, protein 44g, carbs 77g, fat 33g, sat fat 11g, fibre 4g, sugar 9g, salt 3.46g

Summer fruit & nut bake

One mixture, all whizzed in the food processor for ease, makes both the base and topping for this bake. You can vary the fruit – try pineapple, mango, or blackberries.

TAKES 1¼–1½ HOURS

● **CUTS INTO 16–24 SLICES**

200g/7oz butter, diced, plus extra for greasing

250g/9oz self-raising flour

50g/2oz ground almonds

300g/10oz golden granulated sugar

50g/2oz desiccated coconut

2 medium eggs

350–450g/12oz–1lb fresh raspberries (or 340g pack frozen)

1 Heat oven to 180C/160C fan/gas 4. Butter an oblong cake tin (about 31 × 17 × 3cm). Tip the flour, ground almonds, butter and sugar into a food processor and whizz just until the butter is evenly distributed – or rub together by hand. Remove 85g of the mix, stir in the coconut and put to one side. Add the eggs to the remaining mixture in the food processor and whizz quickly – or mix with a wooden spoon. It doesn't need to be very smooth.

2 Spread this mixture over the base of the tin, then scatter half the raspberries over the top. Sprinkle with the coconut mixture and bake for 45 minutes. Dot the remaining fruit over the surface and cook for a further 15 minutes, until firm to the touch. Cool in the tin and cut into slices.

PER SLICE (24) 179 kcals, protein 3g, carbs 21g, fat 10g, sat fat 6g, fibre 1g, sugar 12g, salt 0.3g

Cinnamon custard plums

This easy microwave pud makes a perfect fruity treat to tuck into a lunchbox. You can also use peaches or pears for a change.

TAKES 6 MINUTES ● SERVES 1

1 tbsp honey
1 tsp butter
2–3 plums, quartered
few drops vanilla extract
pinch ground cinnamon
2–3 tbsp ready-made custard

1 Put the honey, butter, plums, vanilla extract, cinnamon and 2 teaspoons water in a dish. Cover with cling film, pierce, and microwave for 3 minutes on high.

2 Leave the plums to cool and put in a sealable container. Spoon the custard on top, seal, then chill until needed.

PER SERVING 148 kcals, protein 2g, carbs 22g, fat 7g, sat fat 4g, fibre 1g, sugar 12g, salt 0.13g

Blueberry lemon cake with coconut crumble topping

This sticky, crumbly bake is irresistible! Bake the day before the picnic, cut into squares and serve from the cake tin.

TAKES 1 HOUR ● CUTS INTO 16 SQUARES

300g/10oz butter, softened, plus extra for greasing
425g/15oz caster sugar
zest 1 lemon
6 eggs
250g/9oz self-raising flour
300g/10oz blueberries
200g/7oz desiccated coconut
200g/7oz lemon curd

1 Heat oven to 180C/160C fan/gas 4 and grease and line a 20 × 30cm cake tin. Beat together 250g of the butter with 250g of the sugar and the lemon zest until fluffy. Break up 4 eggs with a fork, then gradually beat them into the butter and sugar mixture, adding a spoonful of flour, if it begins to curdle. Fold in the flour and a third of the blueberries, then spoon into the tin. Flatten the surface, sprinkle over another third of blueberries, and bake for 20 minutes until surface is set.

2 Melt the remaining butter, then stir in the coconut, remaining sugar and beaten eggs. Warm the lemon curd gently in a pan until it is runny.

3 After the initial baking, scatter the remaining blueberries over the top of the cake, drizzle over the lemon curd, and crumble over the coconut mixture. Bake for a further 20–25 minutes until coconut is golden. Cool, then cut into 16 squares.

PER SQUARE 446 kcals, protein 5g, carbs 50g, fat 27g, sat fat 17g, fibre 3g, sugar 34g, salt 0.55g

Apricot, pecan & choc-chip loaf

This is a good picnic cake as it is moist but firm enough not to get squashed.
The apricots add a good flavour and the nuts add crunch.

TAKES 1 HOUR 20 MINUTES

● **CUTS INTO 12 SLICES**

100g/3½oz softened butter, plus extra
   for greasing
100g/3½oz ready-to-eat dried apricots
150ml/¼ pint unsweetened orange
   juice
100g/3½oz light muscovado sugar
2 eggs
100g/3½oz ground almonds
175g/6oz self-raising flour
3 tbsp milk
50g/2oz choc chips
85g/3oz pecan nut halves
icing sugar, for dusting

1 Heat oven to 180C/160C fan/gas 4. Butter and line the base of a 1.2-litre loaf tin. Chop the apricots and simmer in a small pan with the orange juice for 5 minutes. Allow to cool. Put the butter, sugar, eggs, almonds, flour and milk in a bowl and beat until smooth. Stir in the apricots, the choc chips and two-thirds of the pecans.

2 Spoon into the loaf tin and smooth the top. Scatter over the remaining pecans and bake for 50–60 minutes until firm to the touch and a skewer pushed into the centre comes out clean. Cool for 5 minutes in the tin, then turn out on to a wire rack and dust with icing sugar. Leave to cool completely, then wrap tightly in foil. (Keeps for up to a week, or can be frozen for up to 2 months.)

PER SLICE 307 kcals, protein 6g, carbs 28g, fat 20g, sat fat 6g, fibre 2g, sugar 16g, salt 0.36g

Raspberry & white chocolate traybake

This delicious dessert has the most wonderful texture. It will keep in the fridge for up to three days – leave it in the tin to transport to the picnic.

TAKES 40 MINUTES ● CUTS INTO 16 SQUARES

375g pack ready-rolled shortcrust pastry
flour, for dusting
500g tub mascarpone
100g/3½oz golden caster sugar
100g/3½oz ground almonds
2 eggs
250g/9oz fresh raspberries
100g/3½oz white chocolate, roughly chopped

1 Heat oven to 160C/140C fan/gas 3. Roll out the pastry a little more on a floured surface and use to line a 30 × 20cm tin, or a Swiss roll tin. Line with baking paper, fill with baking beans and cook for 10 minutes. Remove the beans and paper, then return to the oven for a further 5 minutes.

2 Whisk together the mascarpone, sugar, almonds and eggs until well blended. Fold in the raspberries and chocolate, then pour into the tin. Bake for 20–25 minutes until just set and lightly golden. Turn off the oven, open the door and leave the traybake to cool gradually. For the best results, chill for at least 1 hour before slicing.

PER SQUARE 314 kcals, protein 5g, carbs 19g, fat 25g, sat fat 12g, fibre 2g, sugar 13g, salt 0.18g

Squidgy muesli bars

These yummy low-fat bars are easy to make and a healthy choice for lunchboxes.
Bake a batch and freeze or store in an airtight tin for up to a week.

TAKES 30 MINUTES • MAKES 12

100g/3½oz olive oil spread, plus extra
   for greasing
150g/6oz light muscovado sugar
50g/2oz clear honey
300g/10oz high-fibre cereal
50g/2oz mixed dried fruit, chopped
1 tbsp golden linseed or sesame seeds

1 Heat oven to 180C/160C fan/gas 4. Grease and line a 2.5cm-deep, 18cm-square cake tin with rice paper (don't use baking parchment as it dissolves into the muesli bar).

2 Put the sugar, olive oil spread and honey in a large bowl and microwave on high (800W) for 2 minutes. Stir to mix together well. Stir in the high-fibre cereal and the mixed fruit. Spoon into the prepared tin, then flatten the top with the back of a spoon. Sprinkle over the linseed or sesame seeds. Bake for 20 minutes until golden brown.

3 Leave to cool in the tin for at least 30 minutes, then cut into 12 bars. Wrap in greaseproof paper and store.

PER BAR 237 kcals, protein 3g, carbs 36g, fat 10g, sat fat 2g, fibre 2g, sugar 23g, salt 0.05g

Choc–cherry muffins

If you're not keen on cherries, swap them with the same quantity of chopped, ready-to-eat dried apricots or raisins. These muffins freeze well for up to a month.

TAKES 40 MINUTES ● MAKES 12

250g/9oz self-raising flour
1 tsp bicarbonate of soda
140g/5oz dried sour cherries
100g bar white chocolate, cut into chunks
100g bar dark chocolate, cut into chunks
100g/3½oz golden caster sugar
2 eggs, beaten
150g pot natural yogurt
100g/3½oz butter, melted

1 Heat oven to 200C/180C fan/gas 6 and line a 12-hole muffin tin with some paper cases. Sift the flour and bicarbonate of soda into a large bowl, then stir in the cherries, chocolates and sugar. Add the beaten eggs, yogurt and then the butter and stir to combine. It doesn't matter if the mixture looks a bit lumpy, it's more important not to overmix it or the muffins will turn out tough.

2 Fill the paper cases and bake for 20–25 minutes until risen and golden brown. Transfer to a wire rack to cool.

PER MUFFIN 386 kcals, protein 5g, carbs 45g, fat 13g, sat fat 6g, fibre 1g, sugar 18g, salt 0.73g

Biscuity lime pie

The crisp, gingery base is the perfect foil for the zingy citrus filling. Leave in the tin if you're planning to transport this pie.

TAKES 1 HOUR ● SERVES 6

300g pack gingernut biscuits
100g/3½oz butter, melted
3 egg yolks
50g/2oz golden caster sugar
zest and juice 4 limes, plus thin lime
    slices, to decorate
zest and juice 1 lemon
397g can sweetened condensed milk

1 Heat oven to 180C/160C fan/gas 4. Tip the biscuits into a food processor and blitz to crumbs. Add the butter and pulse to combine. Tip the mix into a fluted rectangular tart tin, about 10 × 34cm (or a 20cm-round tin), and press into the base and up the sides right to the edge. Bake for 15 minutes until crisp.

2 While the base is baking, tip the egg yolks, sugar, lime and lemon zests into a bowl and beat with an electric whisk until doubled in volume. Pour in the condensed milk, beat until combined, then add the citrus juices.

3 Pour the mix into the tart case and bake for 20 minutes until just set with a slight wobble in the centre. Leave to set completely, then remove from tin, cool and chill. Serve sliced and topped with the thin lime slices.

PER SERVING 633 kcals, protein 10g, carbs 85g, fat 30g, sat fat 15g, fibre 1g, sugar 64g, salt 0.93g

Raspberry Bakewell cake

Baking the raspberries inside the cake makes this easy to carry to a picnic. This recipe is a great way of using up pick-your-own raspberries.

TAKES 1 HOUR ● SERVES 8

140g/5oz butter, softened, plus extra
    for greasing
140g/5oz ground almonds
140g/5oz golden caster sugar
140g/5oz self-raising flour
2 eggs
1 tsp vanilla extract
250g/9oz raspberries
2 tbsp flaked almonds
icing sugar, to dust

1 Heat oven to 180C/160C fan/gas 4 and base-line and grease a deep, 20cm-round, loose-bottomed cake tin. Blitz the ground almonds, butter, sugar, flour, eggs and vanilla extract in a food processor until well combined.

2 Spread half the mix into the cake tin and smooth the top. Scatter the raspberries over, then dollop the remaining cake mixture on top and roughly spread – you might find this easier to do with your fingers. Scatter with flaked almonds and bake for 50 minutes until golden. Cool, remove from the tin and dust with icing sugar to serve.

PER SERVING 411 kcals, protein 8g, carbs 35g, fat 28g, sat fat 10g, fibre 3g, sugar 21g, salt 0.5g

Sticky plum flapjack bars

Plums have a wonderful flavour but only a short season, so make the most of them while they're in the shops and look out for different varieties at farmers' markets.

TAKES 1 HOUR 20 MINUTES
- **MAKES 18**

450g/1lb fresh plums, halved, stoned and roughly sliced
½ tsp ground mixed spice
300g/10oz light muscovado sugar
350g/12oz butter, plus extra for greasing
300g/10oz rolled porridge oats (not jumbo)
140g/5oz plain flour
50g/2oz chopped walnut pieces
3 tbsp golden syrup

1 Heat oven to 200C/180C fan/gas 6. Tip the plums into a bowl. Toss with the spice, 50g of the sugar and a small pinch of salt, then set aside.

2 Gently melt the butter in a pan. In a large bowl, mix the oats, flour, walnut pieces and remaining sugar together, then stir in the butter and syrup until everything is combined.

3 Grease a 20cm-square baking tin. Press half the oaty mix into the tin, then tip over the plums and spread to make an even layer. Press the remaining oat mixture over the plums so they are completely covered, right to the sides of the tin. Bake for 45–50 minutes until dark golden and starting to crisp a little around the edges. Leave to cool completely, then cut into 18 bars. (These will keep in an airtight container for around 2 days.)

PER BAR 335 kcals, protein 3g, carbs 38g, fat 20g, sat fat 11g, fibre 2g, sugar 22g, salt 0.34g

Cherry & almond slice

If you like Bakewell tart, you'll love this delicious almond-flavoured traybake. It's easy to bake and even easier to eat!

TAKES 1 HOUR • CUTS INTO 15 SLICES

375g pack ready-rolled shortcrust pastry
100g/3½oz butter, softened
100g/3½oz golden caster sugar
1 egg, beaten
25g/1oz ground rice
50g/2oz ground almonds
50g/2oz desiccated coconut
50g/2oz walnuts, roughly chopped
5 tbsp cherry jam
100g/3½oz glacé cherries

1 Heat oven to 180C/160C fan/gas 4 and line the base of an 18 × 27cm baking tin with greaseproof paper. Line the base and sides with the pastry, trim the edges, then chill while you make the filling.

2 Beat the butter and sugar together until fluffy, then gradually add the egg until creamy. Stir in the ground rice, almonds, coconut and nuts. Spread the jam over the pastry, then dollop the almond mix on top. Don't worry if there are some little gaps as the filling will spread during baking. Dot the cherries over the top, then bake for 40–45 minutes until light golden and set. Check after 30 minutes – if the top is browning too quickly, cover loosely with greaseproof paper. Cool in the tin, then cut into slices.

PER SLICE 275 kcals, protein 3g, carbs 27g, fat 18g, sat fat 8g, fibre 1g, sugar 15g, salt 0.36g

Cinnamon berry granola bars

Great for lunchboxes, breakfast on the run or just with a cup of coffee. These will keep for up to a week in an airtight tin.

TAKES 45 MINUTES • MAKES 12

100g/3½oz butter, plus extra for
  greasing
200g/7oz porridge oats
100g/3½oz sunflower seeds
50g/2oz sesame seeds
50g/2oz chopped walnuts
3 tbsp honey
100g/3½oz light muscovado sugar
1 tsp ground cinnamon
100g/3½oz dried cranberries, cherries
  or blueberries, or a mix

1 Heat oven to 160C/140C fan/gas 3. Butter and line the base of an 18 × 25cm tin. Mix the oats, seeds and nuts in a roasting tin, then put in the oven for 5–10 minutes to toast.

2 Meanwhile, warm the butter, honey and sugar in a pan, stirring until the butter is melted. Add the oat mix, cinnamon and dried fruit, then mix until all the oats are well coated. Tip into the tin, press down lightly, then bake for 30 minutes. Cool in the tin, then cut into 12 bars.

PER BAR 294 kcals, protein 6g, carbs 30g, fat 17g, sat fat 6g, fibre 3g, sugar 17g, salt 0.14g

Almond tart with raspberries

This mouthwatering tart is best carried to a picnic in its tin. Pack the raspberries in a separate box and tumble them over the tart to serve.

TAKES 1 HOUR 10 MINUTES, PLUS CHILLING ● **SERVES 4–6**

FOR THE PASTRY

140g/5oz plain flour

85g/3oz cold unsalted butter, cut into cubes

4 tbsp icing sugar

1 egg yolk

FOR THE FILLING

100g/3½oz unsalted butter, softened

100g/3½oz caster sugar

100g/3½oz blanched whole almonds

1 egg

450g/1lb raspberries

1 Pulse the flour and butter for the pastry with a pinch of salt in a food processor to coarse breadcrumbs. Add the icing sugar and egg yolk, then pulse. Remove, wrap in cling film, and chill.

2 Heat oven to 200C/180C fan/gas 6. Coarsely grate the pastry into a 23cm-round, loose-bottomed fluted tin, and press it evenly on to the sides and base. Line with baking parchment, then fill with baking beans and bake blind for 10–12 minutes until very light brown. Remove and leave to cool. Reduce oven temperature to 160C/140C fan/gas 3.

3 Beat together the butter and sugar until pale and light. Chop the almonds in a food processor until fine. Add the butter and sugar, and blend, then add in egg. Spoon into the pastry case and bake for 40 minutes. Cool the tart in its tin on a wire rack, then remove and put on a plate. Top with the raspberries.

PER SERVING (4) 842 kcals, protein 13g, carbs 76g, fat 56g, sat fat 26g, fibre 6g, sugar 6g, salt 0.10g

Muesli fruit-&-nut bars

These moist, nutty bars are perfect for packed lunches. For the best flavour, choose an unsweetened muesli that's not too fruit-filled.

TAKES 40 MINUTES ● CUTS INTO 12 SLICES

100g/3½oz butter, plus extra for greasing
100g/3½oz light muscovado sugar
4 tbsp golden syrup
100g pack pecan nuts
350g/12oz unsweetened muesli
1 medium ripe banana, mashed

1 Heat oven to 180C/160C fan/gas 4. Butter and line the base of an 18 × 28cm (or 22cm-square) tin with baking parchment. Melt the butter, sugar and syrup in a medium pan on a low heat. Stir until the butter has melted and the sugar has dissolved. Cool slightly.

2 Chop half the nuts. Tip the muesli, banana and chopped nuts into the butter mixture and stir until well covered. Spoon into the prepared tin and press down with the back of the spoon until firmly packed.

3 Scatter with the remaining nuts and press lightly into the mixture. Bake for 20–25 minutes until the muesli turns dark golden and the edges have started to crisp. Leave in the tin until cold, then loosen the edges with a knife. Cut into 12 slices. (They will keep in an airtight container for up to 5 days.)

PER SLICE 330 kcals, protein 5g, carbs 34g, fat 20g, sat fat 5g, fibre 3g, sugar 12g, salt 0.24g

Summer berry fizz tartlets

These easily assembled tartlets combine the summer favourites of strawberries, raspberries, Champagne and clotted cream – irresistible!

TAKES 35–45 MINUTES • MAKES 12 TARTLETS

½ × 375g pack sweet dessert pastry
flour, for dusting
1 egg white, beaten
3 tbsp flaked almonds
3 tbsp golden caster sugar
227g punnet strawberries, preferably small ones
150g punnet raspberries
splash of Champagne
handful mint leaves
113g pot Cornish clotted cream

1 Heat oven to 180C/160C fan/gas 4. Roll out the pastry on a floured surface to the thickness of a £2 coin. Cut out 12 circles of pastry to fit a bun tin, re-rolling trimmings as needed. Line the tin with the pastry rounds, then brush with egg white. Crumble over the almonds and sprinkle over 2 tablespoons of the sugar. Bake for 20–25 minutes until golden and starting to go sticky. Leave to cool.

2 Hull and quarter the strawberries and tip into a container with the raspberries. At the picnic, pour Champagne over the fruits and stir in the mint leaves and the remaining sugar. Fill each tartlet with a small blob of clotted cream and top with a pile of boozy fruit.

PER TARTLET 155 kcals, protein 2g, carbs 10g, fat 12g, sat fat 6g, fibre 1g, sugar 2g, salt 0.10g

Index

Also available from BBC Books and *Good Food*

101 30-minute suppers
101 Barbecues and grills
101 Best-ever chicken recipes
101 Best-ever curries
101 Budget dishes
101 Cakes & bakes
101 Cheap eats
101 Chocolate treats
101 Christmas dishes
101 Cupcakes & small bakes
101 Fish & seafood dishes
101 Fruity puds
101 Healthy eats
101 Italian feasts
101 Hot & spicy dishes
101 Low-fat feasts
101 Meals for two
101 Mediterranean dishes
101 More one-pot dishes
101 More low-fat feasts
101 One-pot dishes
101 Pasta & noodle dishes
101 Recipes for kids
101 Seasonal salads
101 Simple suppers
101 Slow-cooking recipes
101 Soups & sides
101 Speedy suppers
101 Storecupboard suppers
101 Teatime treats
101 Tempting desserts
101 Veggie dishes

For 6,000 recipes you can trust see bbcgoodfood.com

bbcgoodfood.com

Great-value family food

Nutty chicken curry

Easy weeknight suppers

Easy sweet & sour chicken

Smart entertaining

Sea bass with sizzled ginger, chilli & spring onion

Hundreds of desserts

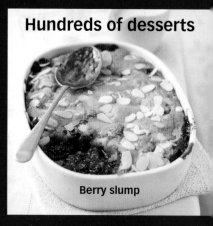

Berry slump

Over 6,000 recipes you can trust